TWAYNE'S WORLD AUTHORS SERIES

A Survey of the World's Literature

Sylvia E. Bowman, Indiana University

GENERAL EDITOR

ITALY

Carlo Golino, University of California

EDITOR

Ludovico Ariosto

(TWAS 301)

TWAYNE'S WORLD AUTHORS SERIES (TWAS)

*The purpose of TWAS is to survey the major writers
—novelists, dramatists, historians, poets, philosophers,
and critics—of the nations of the world. Among the
national literatures covered are those of Australia,
Canada, China, Eastern Europe, France, Germany,
Greece, India, Italy, Japan, Latin America, the Neth-
erlands, New Zealand, Poland, Russia, Scandinavia,
Spain, and the African nations, as well as Hebrew,
Yiddish, and Latin Classical literatures. This survey
is complemented by Twayne's United States Authors
Series and English Authors Series.*

*The intent of each volume in these series is to present
a critical-analytical study of the works of the writer;
to include biographical and historical material that
may be necessary for understanding, appreciation,
and critical appraisal of the writer; and to present all
material in clear, concise English—but not to vitiate
the scholarly content of the work by doing so.*

Ludovico Ariosto

By ROBERT GRIFFIN

University of California, Riverside

Twayne Publishers, Inc. :: New York

Library of Congress Cataloging in Publication Data

Griffin, Robert, 1936–
Ludovico Ariosto.

(Twayne's world authors series, TWAS 301. Italy)
Bibliography: p.
1. Ariosto, Lodovico, 1474–1533.
PQ4599.G68   1974   851′.3   73–15760
ISBN 0–8057–2063–4

MANUFACTURED IN THE UNITED STATES OF AMERICA

To Peter, who can read

Preface

The body of material that Ludovico Ariosto held in his literary memory and the body of scholarship that has been devoted to the *Orlando Furioso* together assume gargantuan proportions.[1] The disproportion between this material and the limitations on this book imposes critical choices. Except for concluding remarks on the impact of the *Furioso* on European literature, and beyond reference in the text to some unusually seminal critical studies, comment on scholarly views will be left to the bibliography. Correspondingly, footnotes will refer more to passages in the *Furioso* related to those under discussion than to the plethora of sources beneath isolated passages. This procedure is in keeping with Ariosto's own notion of the work he was writing, or rather, of the tapestry he was weaving. His episodes never stand by themselves, but rather relate both directly and obliquely to events they follow and foreshadow. Exegesis of the title itself—the hero Orlando who fell madly in love—underlines the plurality of vision in the work to follow, especially when the *Furioso* is measured against some of the one-dimensional medieval works that spawned it. If Ariosto is indebted to Seneca's *Hercules furens* for his title, the debt is only superficial, because so many other sources enter into the world of the poem, become part of its reality, and are transformed by it. Thus, when I have pointed to sources that were unknown to Pio Rajna and others, my purpose has been to illuminate composition of the Ariostan tapestry, not simply to add to the welter of our ever-increasing knowledge of sources.

Unlike Petrarch or Boccaccio, whose Latin works in their time enjoyed a large vogue besides and apart from the works by which they are known to today's larger reading public, Ariosto the writer and the man is apprehensible almost entirely by the great work he nurtured and appeared in. Therefore, his minor works

have been relegated to the brief first part of this book and integrated into the main parts only as they reflect on the *Furioso.*

ROBERT GRIFFIN

University of California

Contents

Chronology

1474 Birth of Ludovico Ariosto on September 8 in Reggio Emilia.

1485 Count Niccolò Ariosto moves his family to Ferrara.

1489 Ludovico begins five years of ill-fated legal studies.

1495 Studies classical Latin authors under Gregorio da Spoleto.

1498 Enters the service of Ercole d'Este.

1500 Death of Niccolò leaves Ludovico responsible for the care of nine brothers and sisters.

1508 Presents *La Cassaria* and writes *I Suppositi* for production the following year.

1509 Goes to Rome to calm the anger of Julius II against Cardinal Ippolito d'Este.

1516 First publication of *Orlando Furioso* (forty cantos).

1517 Declines to accompany Ippolito to Hungary and falls into disfavor. Writes first two satires.

1518 Enters the service of Alfonso d'Este as gentleman-of-the-chamber.

1521 Second edition of *Orlando Furioso*.

1522 Impoverished, Ariosto is named governor of the wild Garfagnana province.

1526– Writes the *Cinque Canti*. Marries Alessandra Benucci se-
1528 cretly in order not to lose ecclesiastical benefices.

1532 Final edition of *Orlando Furioso*, corrected and emended. Goes to Mantua to greet Charles V.

1533 Death of Ludovico Ariosto on July 6.

CHAPTER 1

Along the Pleasant Shore of Italy

(*Orlando Furioso*, XX, 100)

THE political background of Italy during the fifteenth and sixteenth centuries is confusing and disjointed. The peninsula knew little peace and no real unity; its petty kingdoms with their foreign rulers, and the emerging city-states under the firm hand of some eminent family—such as the Medici in Florence, the Sforza in Milan, and the Este in Ferrara—constantly quarrelled and battled. In the wake of the removal of the seat of the papacy and its "captivity" under the protection of the French crown in Avignon (1309–77), the Renaissance popes continued their quest for temporal power and gain. When in 1530 Charles I of Spain led a successful expedition against Italy and was crowned Emperor Charles V of the Holy Roman Empire, practically every remnant of Italian independence withered, and the name *Italia*, despite Machiavelli's dream of unity, became only a geographical designation. Ludovico Ariosto stood on the margin of these events and transmuted their protagonists and place-names into the fitfully heroic world of his great poem.

To find the departure point of so remarkable a development, we must go back to the intervention of Aragon in the affairs of Sicily. Strictly speaking, there was no kingdom of Spain until the marriage of Ferdinand of Aragon and Isabella of Castile (1469). Previously, the Spanish kingdoms had not been strong enough to intervene forcefully in the destiny of Europe. But Aragon had expelled the House of Anjou from Sicily on behalf of a collateral line of its dynasty, had conquered the Balearic Islands, established footholds in Corsica and Sardinia, and established itself in the Kingdom of Naples—a hegemony that Ariosto's Astolfo will approach by sea and survey by air. After 1492 Castile would bring to the marriage the newly discovered Americas. In the Spanish state of Ferdinand and Isabella, religious and political feeling were linked so closely that it was impossible to dissever them. From 1480 the Inquisition became an arm of the state, entrusted with the surveillance of converted Jews and, after the fall of Granada in 1492, of Moslems (*Maranos*); indeed, the strongest reproach that Argalia can make to Ferraú is "mancator di fé, marano" (*Orlando Furioso*, I, 26).[1] While Columbus set out to find a new world to subject and convert, expeditions against the coasts of Morocco, Algeria, and Tunisia seemed to announce that all the forces of Spain were about to league themselves against Islam. War against the Moors had absorbed all Spanish energies until the middle of the thirteenth century, and the common memory two centuries later was the memory of the Christian Crusade. The Holy War, long interrupted, was resumed against the Moors, so that the final constitution of the national territory seemed no less than the result of a Crusade. Spain would have won no greater glory and ascendancy than to make herself the champion of the Church and of Europe in the face of the Turkish threat, magnified by the fall of Constantinople in 1453 and the subsequent taking of many prisoners on Christian soil from the time of Mohammed II.[2] Yet she turned aside from the Holy War with the Crescent to protect the dynastic ambitions of her princes on the Christian Continent.

Dynastic ambition was also at work in Northern Italy, while vacillation reshaped the fate of the Southern tip of the peninsula. When Giangaleazzo Visconti died in 1402, his expanding Milanese state broke up, but it had lasted long enough to alarm Venice. The merchant republic therefore embarked on a policy of landward expansion and proceeded to seize a large part of Eastern Lombardy. In the meantime, Florence set out to conquer Tuscany. After half a century of warfare all of Italy north of the Papal States was divided between Venice, Milan, and Florence, with smaller states maintaining a precarious existence among them. For the next forty years Italy witnessed the first example of consciously calculated balance-of-power politics in the history of modern Europe, an unstable equilibrium manipulated by these states, together with the papacy and the Kingdom of Naples, to prevent domination by a single state. By the sixteenth century balance of power began to swing in the direction of the dynastic imperialism of the Hapsburgs, whose control over lands as widely separated as Spain and Bohemia would eventually dominate the map of Europe and the diplomacy of its states (cf. *OF*, XV, 23, 32). But at the turn of the century Naples remained a bone of contention.

After having acknowledged as her successor Alfonso the Great of Aragon, a distant relative of the Este family, Queen Joanna of Naples bequeathed her crown to René of Anjou, who in turn transferred his claim on Naples to the House of France. In 1494 Charles VIII, seeking adventure and dreaming of glory, crossed the Alps. With the heart of a knight-errant and the brain of a simple fool, he marched through an astonished Italy to assume his crown "in bold emulation of the emperor of Constantinople," as his official annalist put it. It was a strange campaign. Rallied by the cry "Dieu est avec nous!," Commines tells us, he conquered Italy with wooden spurs and triumphantly led a powerful army that fought no battles. The invasion and subjection of Italy from 1494 through the next generation resulted not only from the inability of the Italian states to unite permanently against the foreigner, but also from their having left the business of warfare to mercenaries and thus from their having lost the art of self-defense. Repulsed the following year by a coalition directed by the Pope and comprised of Milan, Venice, and ultimately Spain, Charles VIII was followed in 1499 by Louis XII, who claimed not only Naples but, as a descendant of Valentino Visconti, also Milan, which he held for over a decade. In 1511 again a Pope, this time Julius II, successfully united Venice (for its own protection), Ferdinand, and eventually Emperor Maximilian of Austria and Henry VIII of England (for their political advantage), against the French claimant.[3] In the machinations and flux of alliances made, broken, and remade, Ferrara supported French intervention because of the single bond of common enemies: Venice and Rome. Down through the history of Ferrara these two contending powers had been and would continue to be the predominant forces counteracting on the development of that city-state until the close of the sixteenth century. Concerned with controlling the Adriatic and policing the entrance to the Po against possible Turkish advance, Venetian Terraferma had expanded to the loss of Ferrara. The marriage of Isabella d'Este and Francesco Gonzaga further tied Ferrara to Mantua, another victim and sworn enemy of Venetian expansion. Moreover, Julius II, like Sixtus IV before him, had aimed at bringing Ferrara under his control, until Alfonso d'Este and the French won their Pyrrhic victory over the combined forces of the papacy and Spain at Ravenna in 1512. The final French invasion occurred in 1515, now headed by Francis I, and now in league with Venice. Italy was thus reduced primarily to the dominance of two great powers: Spain in the South and France in the Northwest, while central Italy was in the hands of the Medici family and Venice regained control of the Northeast. This ebb and flow of power, pledges betrayed, honor sacrificed to self-interest, would all characterize Italian politics and war for decades. And the following year Ariosto published the *Orlando Furioso*.

I *Ferrara*

Reacting against the biographical misuse of a writer's work which was very common four decades ago, certain critics in recent years have attempted to rule out biography from the criticism of literature. We must divorce the literary work from its creator, the argument runs, and while this has led, in a very healthy way, to an insistence upon the importance of a writer's text, it has also led to the view that the literary work is a mere artifact, to be examined as we would a vase or an ancient ornament in a museum. A work cannot be redissolved into a life, yet it can offer us something of the texture of that life and of the life of the mind, which is what the literary life really is. Ariosto's mind and emotions were, of course, distinct from the lives of the soldiers and rulers whom he entertained, in whose shadow he lived, and whose intellectual attainments were not written out day after day upon sheets of paper in a study, but were lived out in a parliament or on a battlefield. Perhaps more than any other writer of his time, however, Ariosto's literary voice is not one of the "voices of silence" and will require extensive comment in later chapters; it cannot be separated as easily as might be believed either from the speaker or from the listening world in which he moved. His life is inextricably woven—to use his own word—into the lives of the great Este lords whose whims he served, whose praise he sang, and whose fame he equalled or surpassed in another sphere; any account of Ariosto's life, then, must to a considerable extent be a summary history of the Este family. His major and minor works alike are informed by a Renaissance humanism of which he is an unexcelled exemplar and which in some respects he held in contempt. Thus, they mirror the complex ambivalence of his time, an ambivalence to which none lends itself so well as his richly illuminating idiom. Such a portentous claim is all the more remarkable when we realize through hindsight that the poet's birth date in 1474 coincided with or shortly preceded the birth of such Northern Italian figures as Michelangelo, Castiglione, Guicciardini, Raphael, Andrea del Sarto, Correggio, and Aretino. The Ariosti were originally a Bolognese family of minor nobles, whose fortunes increased when they reestablished themselves in Ferrara in the fourteenth century. Through the marriage of the undistinguished Obizzo III and Lippa Ariosto, "La bella Lippa da Bologna," as she was later praised (*OF*, XIII, 73), the Ariosti became affiliated with the Este family, which Ludovico was later to eternalize in the persons of Ippolito, Alfonso I, the Ercoles, and Isabella.

Present-day Ferrara is attended by the melancholy memory of the sumptuous, lettered, and artistic court of the Estensi princes. The contemporary visitor who walks the Corso Giovecca toward Montagnuola or the Corso Ercole d' Este toward the Castello Estense with its delicate balustrades, high crenelated towers, and deep moat might experience the feeling of loss that the Renaissance observer felt before the ruins of Rome. The once celebrated university is no longer in evidence, but the Sala dell' Aurora in the Castle still contains the paintings of Dosso Dossi which represent the hours of the day, surrounded by marble benches recalling the last celebrations of the Este court. At a short remove from the Castle, the Sala dei Mesi in the Palazzo Schifanoia (literally: "carefree") displays scenes from the life of Borso d'Este on its peeling walls. These empty rooms and still-life scenes barely intimate the vibrant life of dark passions and high attainments that characterized the Este family in the fifteenth century, near the end of which Ferrara reached a population of around a hundred thousand inhabitants and thus attained parity with Florence, Milan, and Venice. In his first comedy one of Ariosto's characters succinctly describes a thinly disguised Ferrara as "a wise city that intends to increase in state" and, with a casual swipe at clerical abuse, wryly declares the obligation of its citizens to oversee its direction (*La Cassaria*, I, v). Fifteenth-century archival records, which contrast the black death of early generations with the end of the century when there were no houses available for rent, suggest that Ferrara grew to challenge its own resources.[4] Between these two extremes Leonello and Borso, the two illegitimate sons of Niccolò, competed for power, yet both were beneficent administrators and enlightened Maecenases. They sponsored painting as Niccolò before them had encouraged Van der Weyden and Pisanello. The first, and perhaps the most notable, Este ruler during Ariosto's life was Niccolò's son Ercole I (1431–1505), an extremely intelligent and competent governor who had numerous churches and monasteries built during his reign. He also attempted to have his nephew and rival, Niccolò di Leonello, poisoned. He married his mistress Eleanor of Aragon who, during her husband's absence, succeeded in putting down an attempted coup by Niccolò. Captured and decapitated, the latter was buried in a solemn ceremony that witnessed the hypocritical laments of Eleanor and her court. Later, according to rumor, he poisoned his wife on learning that she was going to poison him. Although his personal history was violent and bloody, his government of the city was generally respected and even revered by his subjects. Ercole and his two famous daughters, Beatrice and Isabella, moreover encouraged the arts and sciences. It was during the tenure of Ercole, when Dias and Columbus, and a little later da Gama and Magellan, were bringing about some freedom from prejudice plus a thirst for more knowledge, that the Estensi acquired some of Europe's most notable maps. At a time when the center of the world was shifted from the Mediterranean, the Este maps represented some of Europe's finest Ptolemaic cartography, which was then stirring the minds of Renaissance geographers.

It was also during the tenure of Ercole that Ludovico's father distinguished himself for bravery—that is, as the agent of Ercole in the attempted poisoning of Lionello's son—and received as a reward the command of the citadel at Reggio, two years before the poet's birth on September 8, 1474. A skillful and marginally scrupulous administrator, Niccolò Ariosto assumed various offices as he shuttled his family to and around Reggio in 1481, at that time the home of Matteo Boiardo, and finally to Ferrara in 1485, pressured all along the way by the encroachment of Venetian Terraferma. In the following years, until his death in 1500, Niccolò continued his peregrinations with his family, always winning high office—witness his election to Judge of the Twelve

Sages in 1486—and always drawing questions about his honesty. Though dishonest tax collectors were not uncommon, the charge of financial mismanagement was not a light accusation in this city which, more than any other of the time, constantly needed public funds to hire mercenaries and to shore up its already imposing fortifications. Around this time Ludovico began to receive lessons at home from Domenico Catabene, a student of jurisprudence, and shortly thereafter from the humanist Luca Ripa, tutor of Ercole and Tito Strozzi, and finally from Giovanni Sadoleto, a notary and professor of jurisprudence. The conflict in Ariosto's life between the study of law, which Niccolò had outlined for his son's future in business administration, and the study of belles lettres, was to be short-lived. During the formal years of his law studies (1489–94) he was more actively pursuing what would become a lifelong interest in the theater, participating as an actor in the numerous Italian versions of the comedies of Plautus and Terence, and as an aspiring author, perhaps of a now lost *Tragedia di Tisbe*, in the productions and official celebrations desired by Duke Ercole. The court of Ferrara had been the first among the Italian courts to take a serious interest in dramatic art. It possessed a permanent stage and a huge stock of flesh-colored tights for dancers and danseuses. Ferrara had seen the first Italian stage-play, the *Favola di Cefalo* of Niccolò da Correggio. A tale frequently told to illustrate the young poet's flair for the dramatic is that of an upbraiding he received at the hands of his father for his supposedly dissolute life. His younger brother Gabriele was struck by the penitent silence of Ludovico, not realizing that he was mentally fashioning the paternal lecture into a dramatic set piece for a comedy he was then formulating (*La Cassaria*, V, ii), and was too bemused by the theatrical situation to protest his real innocence.[5] Although undoubtedly apocryphal, the story bespeaks an imitative faculty we will find at work in the *Furioso*.

The next phase of Ariosto's education was more initiation than training, when he began the study of Latin authors under the guidance of the humanist Augustinian friar Gregorio da Spoleto (1495). The eager pupil became so proficient that he opened the studio in the fall of that year with a traditional Latin oration. Presently he was to study under the direction of the Platonist Sebastiano dall' Aquila, and finally at the turn of the century under his near-contemporary Pietro Bembo. Ariosto wrote the majority of his Latin poems in these years, but the humanistic idyll was soon to become clouded by more mundane preoccupations. When Niccolò Ariosto died in 1500, he left his oldest son, not yet twenty-six years old, in charge of four younger brothers and five sisters, not to mention a confused and worsening financial situation and legal complications arising from the father's bequeathed and partly squandered legacy. Ludovico's initiation into the ways of the world had already begun, in a sense, with his entry into the service of Ercole d'Este early in 1498. This was the beginning of a long, taxing, and disillusioning personal service at the Este court, and made of Ariosto's life an almost classic example of the conflicting tugs felt by many Renaissance poets between the disinterested calling of one's muse and the obligation to ennoble the intrigue and pragmatic actions of one's patron.[6] This is the tension we read between the lines of the poem written to the profligate Ippolito d' Este in praise of his chastity (*Carmina*, II, 2), and of the epithalamium he wrote for the twice-married Lucrezia Borgia in 1502, whom he celebrated as a "most beautiful virgin"—a tension that is entirely absent from, say, Bembo's eulogy of the blond, beautiful, and charming Lucrezia in the *Asolani*. Despite his having developed Ferrara into an exemplary Renaissance city with a sense of urban community, Ercole was something less than generous with the artists and artisans who individually contributed to this accomplishment. Ludovico's early maturity was thus a paradigm for the famous Ariostan irony that centuries of critics would later voluminously discuss.

This legacy of responsibilities and cares pushed Ariosto further into the service of the Estensi and moved him to seek and accept the post of Capitain of the Rocca of Canossa. The appointment allowed the small pleasure of occasional visits to his native Reggio and to his mother's family living there. His burden was not lightened by the birth of his first illegitimate son a year later in 1503, the result of a brief liaison with his servant Maria, so he assumed minor orders as a means of augmenting his funds through a trickle of resulting ecclesiastical benefices—a blessing that would be mixed with complications and squabbles in later years—and entered the household of Ippolito. Ariosto's poetry of this period is interesting for his ability to fantasize some of the bloody deeds of the Este family. The *Capitoli* I, "Canterò l'arme, canterò gli affanni" (1504), the sketch of a heroic poem in *terzine* on the enigmatic Obizzo d'Este, is notable in this respect for the echo of chivalric romance it will bring to the *Orlando Furioso*, which he was about to begin writing. Especially notable is the first eclogue (1506), which under the guise of shepherds in Arcadia treats the conjuration and horrors of the accession to power of Ippolito and Alfonso I, who blinded and imprisoned their half-brother Giulio. The gist of the work was to claim that Giulio was the son of a dissolute courtier and thus to deny him a place in the chain of succession from Ercole. The eclogue does not touch on the widespread rumor that Ippolito gouged out Giulio's eyes because they caught the fancy of Angela Borgia, with whom Ippolito was ardently infatuated.

Of a more practical bent were the minor and major diplomatic missions assigned to him, at first within reach of the Este family tree and its landholdings. Initially, he was sent by Ippolito to Lucrezia d'Este, the wife of Annibale Bentivoglio of Bologna, and then to the wife of Francesco Gonzaga of Mantua, Isabella, who would figure prominently in the *Orlando Furioso* and would remain his literary confidant during the poem's initial stage of composition. After a minor interlude of calm during which he translated some Latin comedies, oversaw the premiere of his *Cassaria*, and set about writing *I Suppositi*, he was sent to Rome on a much more delicate assignment. Having betrayed the League of Cambray, in 1510 Julius II was maturing his offensive against the French, Venice was won over, and everything seemed ready, when he fell at odds with Alfonso I, who had elected a French alliance. The fury of Julius was unbounded and it broke out in a dispute over some revenues due to the Holy See, the result of Ippolito's having forcibly assumed the priorate at Nonantola, of which the Pope made a pretext for exacting the alliance of Ferrara to the Church. Thundering an excommunication against Alfonso, he concentrated his armaments on one object: "Ferrara, t'avrò pel corpo di Dio." His narrow patriotic vision became all the more intense, for Ferrara was the mote in his eye, the traitor, the backslider, and he saw no further. Ariosto was entrusted not only to explain the French alliance to the angry Pope, but also to arrange a meeting among the three principals. This was the first of various diplomatic trips to represent Ferrarese interests, primarily against the Venetians, at the papal court of Julius, who once threatened to throw Ariosto into the Tiber, as he had done to others, if he did not leave immediately. On the death of Pope Julius, he continued diplomatic missions to the court of his former acquaintance, the Medici Leo X, from whom he vainly sought greater diplomatic concessions and personal consideration. In the interstice between these trips and actual participation in the fighting against Venice, his second and favorite son, Virginio, was born to a certain Orsolina Sassomarina and received his father's affection, doting care, and companionship throughout his life.

From this period date the two consuming loves of Ariosto's life. In June of 1513 he met another old acquaintance in Florence, Alessandra Benucci, and declared a love that was shared and did not wane over the next twenty years. Despite the death of her husband Tito Strozzi in 1515, the couple was not married until some dozen years later, and then only secretly in order to maintain the small ecclesiastical revenue that Ludovico was intermittently receiving, or else to safeguard Alessandra's legacy from her first marriage. The second sustaining love, the *Orlando Furioso*, was finally published in 1516 after much pruning and polishing. These pressing concerns were more than enough to occupy his life at Ferrara. Consequently, when Cardinal Ippolito, Archbishop of Gran and Primate of Hungary since the age of seven and newly appointed Bishop of Buda, decided to transfer his entourage to Hungary, Ludovico respectfully but firmly exposed his reasons for wishing to remain at home. As a reward for his candor, Ippolito brusquely dismissed him from his service.

Thus ended an eventful episode in Ariosto's life, and so began an equally eventful one the following year when he entered the service, in roughly the same capacity, of Alfonso I. His life, therefore, was not markedly changed. But whereas Ippolito had no ear for poetry, was no patron of the arts, and undertook, at least in the case of the trip to Hungary, travel for self-aggrandizement, Alfonso enjoyed travel throughout Europe for the purpose of both practical education and personal enrichment. Shortly after entering the household of his new patron, Ariosto was thus able to devote some leisure to all aspects—satire, drama, and, of course, the *Furioso*—of his literary corpus abuilding, although his perpetual round of menial administrative tasks may have been his stimulus to complete his unfinished work. In 1521 he issued a new edition of his poem, still in forty cantos. Until the administration of Alfonso, Ferrara had been one of the few Italian cities not to delay payment of wages to its soldiers and professors alike by so much as one day. But the continued threat of war with Leo X, following so shortly the military spending incurred by the struggle with Julius II and Venice, forced the duke to delay and even suspend the poet's pay. Financial affairs failed to improve when Ariosto's cousin died intestate, leaving in question the ownership of substantial property holdings; the Ariosti brought suit, but since they were in effect suing the duke himself, who was sorely pressed for money, nothing came of their action. This bitter situation will find its comic mirror image in Ariosto's *La Lena* (IV, iii) some seven or eight years later. In turn, Ariosto was forced in the winter of 1522 to accept the governorship of the Garfagnana district in the Apennines, which the Estensi now controlled. Their acquisition was no triumph and his appointment was no promotion, albeit it was a testimony to Alfonso's faith in Ludovico's administrative talents and strength of character, for the area was the least productive in the Este domain, was dotted with treacherous passes and infested with bandits. His three-year-long dealings with the recalcitrant populace of this area justify the confidence invested in him and speak well of his lawgiving and peacemaking attributes. At the very least they belie the fanciful portrait frequently drawn of a gentle though absentminded poet, preoccupied with a nonexistent world, which coincides, but for the wrong reasons, with the portrait he draws of "himself" in the *Furioso*; his life can be romanced only by overlooking the tedium and servitude that marked most of it.[7] Yet his last four satires written at this time recall the elegiac laments of Ovid in exile from civilization. He declined an ambassadorship to the court of Clement VII, and in 1525 returned to Ferrara, never again to leave for any length of time the real center of his world to which he was always drawn.

Ariosto's last years seem to have been the most tranquil and rewarding of his life. In a sense, his life had come full circle. For the first time in a quarter of a century money appears not to have been a controlling factor in his life. Over the years he had given ample proof of his diplomatic and administrative talents, and so in 1528 he was elected, as his father had been over forty years earlier, to the post of Judge of the Twelve Sages. Perhaps even more gratifying was his appointment as director of theatrical construction and production at the Este court, a position which enabled him to attend to his own dramatic works and adapt them to his changing notions of dramatic style. He closed out his career as a playwright in 1531 by producing a revised version of his initial effort, *La Cassaria.* These new assignments (e.g., production of *La Lena*) and his growing stature at court brought him in contact with such figures as the bride of Ercole II, Renée de France, whose intellectual interests and clear Protestant leanings would soon attract to Ferrara Calvin and Marot, and ultimately some of the turmoil that was to sweep through Europe. In the same vein of prestigious accomplishment were his last diplomatic trips to representatives of Ferrara's temporary enemies. In 1531 he was received with pomp and flourish in Modena by Alfonso de Avalos, the head of a visiting Spanish force, and the next year he presented a copy of the final edition of the *Orlando Furioso* to Charles V, Holy Roman Emperor and Grand Master of the Order of the Golden Fleece, who incarnated the aspirations and failures of sixteenth-century knighthood; the scene bore ironies that even Ariosto might not have imagined. Finally, this poet who enjoyed travelling only in the "zodiac of his own wit" retired to his *parva domus,* which today can be seen in a considerably restored state in the Via Mirasole. The uncertain date of his death, which is generally placed around July 6, 1533, and the absence of ceremony at his burial are accurate commentaries on the solitude of his last days, a solitude he was denied most of his life. His body is now interred in the Biblioteca Ariostea of Ferrara beneath a large marble tomb supplied by Napoleon.

CHAPTER 2

Minor Works

At the falling of the curtain would appear,
amid a thousand lights, the stage.

(*Orlando Furioso*, XXXII, 80)

A RIOSTO'S Latin and Italian poetry, his satires, and especially his comedies, can be classed as minor works only because they are overshadowed by the prodigious reach of the *Furioso*. His venture into the theater falls after but is an extension of one of the fundamental revolutions of the Renaissance, the invention and spread of printing (ca. 1440–50). Besides the vernacular Bible, it made comparatively cheap and easy the acquisition of texts like the dozen new plays of Plautus discovered by Nicholas of Cusa in 1428, and greatly increased the number of people who could read these works and who could thus enjoy hearing them recited in centers of interest in the theater like Ferrara. Sermons preached in that city in mid-fifteenth century against an excessive devotion to the plays of Terence indicate not only a precocious and pronounced taste for Roman comedy, but also a new attitude toward purified classical comedy. As late as Poliziano's *Favola di Orfeo* (1471) classical subjects were occasionally still set in medieval religious staging. Shortly after the time when Guarino was adding to the recently published commentaries by Donatus on Terence which were to guide dramatic theory for years to come, the *Menaechmi* and *Amphitruo* of Plautus and the *Andria* of Terence were performed in Latin for the Este court during Ariosto's youth, and soon followed by the *Eunuchus, Captivi, Trinummus, Mercator, Asinaria,* and others. While humanists attempted to resurrect to the letter the conventions of Roman comedy, and initiated controversy that would rage as late as Daniello and Trissino as to whether comedy should have *intermezzi*, the Estensi were sponsoring dramatic interludes that all but outshone the tediously translated comedies they were designed to offset. There the Olympian gods and legendary figures that populated humanistic comedies mixed into the combats of Roman warriors and Moorish torch dances.[1] We do not know if the distracted sixteen-year-old law student participated with other young men in the *moresca* that outstripped the performance of *Amphitruo* staged for the marriage of Prince Alfonso and Anna Sforza; he would have taken part in a musical, choral, and panto-mime celebration of a future Hercules issuing from the House of Este. It is almost certain that Ariosto at least witnessed the feast of Alfonso's second marriage, which saw the production of five Plautine comedies in which the same costume was not seen twice on any of the more than one hundred total personae.

His entry into this world as an artist was inauspicious, if we credit his frail and propagandistic *Egloga I* as drama, a designa-tion that might not have been questioned a century earlier, or even if we follow other critics and biographers in assuming that he had adapted and translated the *Menaechmi* and *Aulularia,* the *Eunuchus, Phormio,* and *Andria.* But from the first words of its prologue *La Cassaria* marks a fresh departure for Italian comedy, even as it points back to specific Roman conventions. "I present New Comedy to you, full of various games which were never recited on stage in Greek or Latin. It seems to me that most are inclined to blame it, as soon as I have said New . . ." Ariosto goes on to defend modern attempts in the vernacular to rival classical eloquence in verse or prose, but the essential point has been made from the outset. He does not intend to stage a new comedy, as it is often assumed, but rather New Comedy itself, the comedy initiated by the legendary Menander and highlighted by Plautus and Terence.

The main material of classical Old Comedy was polemics, political controversy, and personal satire, and it was written for specific occurrences of the day or the hour. On the other hand, in New Comedy contemporary historical background for the most part is superficial, its subject matter is taken almost exclusively from the everyday life of the upper middle class at Athens or Rome, and its characters tend toward the typical. Satire on indi-vidual personalities has passed to the humor of people taken as a class. Plot lines are usually simple, repetitive, and frequently improbable. They involve, for instance, an idler son's need of money for a hard-hearted pimp or for his sweetheart, recognition of her as someone's long-lost daughter, and intrigue that turns on machinations of the clever slave to secure this money from the stupid or irascible father. Stories invariably end with an apology or a reconciliation. Its sons and fathers are very much like sons and fathers of any age, and its milieu of family life is a rich mine of comic material. As the so-called Erudite Comedy initiated by Ariosto, modern Italian comedy follows these prescriptions closely from the prologue through the five acts of exposition of the argument, its development, crisis, proposed solution, and final resolution.[2] With nationalistic traits assigned later by Trissino and others to groups of characters, the French being fickle, Turks wily, and Italians naturally wise, it was inevitable that the theater be an improbable and anachronistic throwback to earlier typologies, and that characters be exaggerated. Since psychological insight was simply not within the conventions of the time, it is at least anachronistic, on the other hand, for modern critics like De Sanctis to chide Ariosto's characters for not being "real."[3] It took an exceptional drama like the *Mandragola* to prove the prevailing rules of cinquecento comedy. But adherence to the dictates of New Comedy and to its urge to update allusions and depict contemporary society was at the same time the salvation of Italian comedy, thus allowing it to escape from the restrictions of purely humanistic comedy. Ariosto and his successors totally incorporated the stock characters of Roman comedy, yet while depiction of a society riddled by vice and corruption outdistanced real conditions, they modified their speech, habits, and setting to bring them within the spectator's sense of affinity and allow him to recognize his neighbor. *Il Negromante* anticipates Lasca in introducing a new comic type, the magician-astrologer, a combined knave and fool who modifies the deceitful friar type that Boccaccio had illustrated so famously and who will recur frequently in European comedy later in this period.

La Cassaria premiered before the Este court during the Carnival festivities of 1508. Superficially, the play is an amalgam of the *Aulularia*, *Mostellaria*, and *Poenulus* of Plautus and the *Andria* and *Heautontimorumenos* of Terence, though it does embody satire of contemporary personalities and society and is the first play in Europe to use modern stage setting. The comedy also reveals strains of the "double plot" for which Terence has been criticized and merges a society of fathers, sons, and servants. It deals with the quandary of two young men, Erofilo and Caridoro, who attempt to liberate a pair of slaves, Eulalia and Corisca, from the pander Lucrano. They set out to do this when Erofilo "borrows" a chest of gold (i.e., *la cassaria*) from his supposedly absent father, Crisobolo, and has his astute servant Trappola give it to Lucrano as collateral for the release of Corisca. This servant, like the other servants in the play, enjoys some of the finest comic lines in the often-quoted recognition scene with Lucrano (III, iii):

TRAPPOLA: Tell me, my good man.
LUCRANO: You surely don't seem to be from these parts, giving me a name which has never graced me nor my father nor any member of my family.
TRAPPOLA: Excuse me, I didn't see you very well. Let me start over. Tell me, my sad man of low birth . . . but, my goodness, you are perhaps the man I am looking for, or his brother, cousin, or at least a relative.
LUCRANO: Could be. And who are you looking for?
TRAPPOLA: A cheat, a liar, a murderer.
LUCRANO: Slow down. You're on the right track. What is his name?
TRAPPOLA: His name . . . he is called . . . I had it on the tip of my tongue; I don't know what I did with it.
LUCRANO: You've either swallowed it or spit it out. [Fig., you're holding back or have actually revealed it.] . . . So pick it up out of the dust.
TRAPPOLA: I can describe him so easily that we won't need his name. He is a blasphemer and liar.
LUCRANO: Those are the traits of my business.
TRAPPOLA: Thief, falsifier, persecutor . . . pimp.
LUCRANO: The main point of my talent.
TRAPPOLA: Informer, slanderer, creator of scandal and quarrels.
LUCRANO: If we were at the Roman Court we wouldn't know who you are looking for, but here in Mitylene you can be looking only for me. I am even going to tell you my name: I am Lucrano.

Erofilo then goes to Caridoro's father to suggest that the gold has been stolen by Lucrano, who thereupon is arrested with the chest in his possession. Everything goes according to Erofilo's design when Lucrano agrees to bestow Corisca if only Caridoro will persuade his father, the chief of police Bassa, to use his influence to have the charges dropped. But the crisis occurs when Trappola is beset by well-intentioned *servi*, who free the girl and deliver her to an astonished Erofilo, whose father is on the point of returning. Volpino, somewhat less a master servant than Trappola, plays on the credulity of Crisobolo by implicating one of the latter's loyal servants, by improbably passing off a disguised Trappola as a merchant and deaf-mute, and nervously persuades him to seek his gold at the house of Lucrano, which he promptly does. Suspicious, Crisobolo returns to hear Trappola's confession and have Volpino bound. But he yields to Fulcio, still another astute servant, who gets Volpino a pardon, hoodwinks both Lucrano and Crisobolo, and receives money from the latter to buy Corisca for Caridoro. The literary memory has no difficulty in recalling kindred scenes from Roman comedy, but the play's true wellsprings are varied and mercurial. Momentarily, dialogue approaches the edge of seriousness on subjects like love, filial duties, and paternal obligations, but then motives lapse back into self-interest. To this extent the actions and impulses of the company of servants mirror an exaggerated picture of the polite society they serve. Ariosto's characters make random jibes at social institutions and at the paramount stress on favorable appearance at court, the representatives of which in the audience surely delighted in the caricature.

The successful initial venture of *La Cassaria* was surpassed by that of *I Suppositi* one year later, at least if we may judge by its premiere and successive performances. We may at least judge how much Ariosto's reputation had grown in the aftermath of his 1516 publication of the *Furioso*. For the 1519 performance before the pontifical court of Leo X and his roughly two thousand guests, Raphael had painted on the curtain especially for the comedy a beautiful city scene in perspective.[4] That city was Ferrara, the locale in which *I Suppositi* is set, and this situation comedy owes much to the trend Ariosto established in 1508. We still have an entanglement of sons and lovers, characters making pointed asides to the spectators about corrupt Italian officials, and an improbable plot mechanized by substitutions of characters —thus one of the explanations of the title. In the quickly paced preface, where the author acknowledges his debt to Plautus and Terence, he allows some bawdy meanings of *Suppositi* and inveighs against Roman vice. Despite his declaration of sources, it is clear that Ariosto has learned as much from his first venture into dramaturgy as from classical texts.

As the play opens we learn that Erostrato, the son of a rich merchant in Catania, has come to study at the University in Ferrara. On his arrival, he immediately fell in love with Polinesta, who has already been promised by her father, Damone, to Cleandro, an old, prosperous, and stuffy doctor of law. In order to pursue his love, Erostrato joins the household staff of Damone in the disguise of his own servant, Dulipo, who in turn replaces his master and attends the university as a man of means and leisure. Dulipo's travesty enables him to outbargain Cleandro for the marriage contract, while a frightened traveller from Siena is pressed into service as the pretended father of the substitute Erostrato and the potential bearer of a large dowry. A complication arises when the real father, Filogono, unexpectedly arrives. When he is turned away by servants at his son's house, confronts his Sienese double, and sees Dulipo in his master's clothes, he immediately suspects him of fraud and seeks a lawyer—Cleandro, of course—to secure the return of Erostrato. In quick succession Damone discovers the ruse of the servant "Dulipo" (Erostrato), whom he orders to be blinded and imprisoned, but Cleandro joyously learns that "Erostrato" (Dulipo) is in fact his long-lost son and heir, who was taken by the Turks during the occupation of Otranto in 1480.[5] Damone's feelings are smoothed over when Erostrato's father agrees to his son's marriage to Polinesta.

As we might suspect, strongly delineated characterization in *I Suppositi* is only intermittent and derivative.[6] The "nurse," who is simply named "Balia" in the rhymed version, is engaging but soon drops from sight, and her mistress Polinesta is only a pretext for launching the plot. If the paternal affection of Filogono rings true, we must thank Terence's Menedemus for serving as his model. The parasite as well, Pasifilo, has a long ancestry in literature; the etymology of his name ("love of everything"), like that of Erofilo ("love of love"), Volpino (the "foxy" one), and Camillo Pocosale ("dimwit") of *Il Negromante*, makes him a recognizable type, common to Plautine comedy, whose dialogue lives up to this single dimension of his personality (cf. I, ii); Pasifilo's name and general traits recall those of Panfilo in Boccaccio's *Fiammetta*. And finally, Cleandro steps in for the *pedante* of the Commedia dell'Arte. The comedy emphasizes the situation of each character at odds with that of the others, rather than their individual emotions; yet, as in the case of the selfish Damone, his daughter's transgression has made him more aware of his own shortcomings. Of greater dramatic interest than sketch of character are the skill Ariosto shows in manipulating situations and his portrayal of contemporary Ferrarese society. Aside from its inherent improbability, the discovery that Dulipo is not only not the person he claims to be but is as well someone he himself did not even suspect lends greater dimension to the title. The play gains a sense of immediacy through the swipes at local officialdom at a level low enough not to bring reprisal against the author, through references to events like the brief but terrifying Turkish occupation of Otranto—as *La Cassaria* had alluded to the forced lodging of occupying Imperial forces—and through its scintillating dialogue.

Despite the manifest success of Ariosto's first two comedies, more than a decade elapsed before he returned to the theater. In a sense, though, he had never left; he continued to oversee production of his extant plays and probably to assist in or personally execute further translations of Roman comedy. Aside from his preoccupation with the adventures of Orlando and his own with Alessandra, he was caught in the turmoil of personal affairs that failed to improve. Beyond those misfortunes previously mentioned, in those days of incunabular editions of popular literature and in the absence of copyright laws Ariosto had also to contend with mangled versions of his plays that had been pirated in 1509. This is one of the explanations he gives us in the preface to the second version of the *Cassaria* for remodeling the play. But there were other reasons for making the play "più bella che mai fosse" ("prettier than ever"). Shortly after the 1519 opening of *I Suppositi* in Rome he plunged into another kind of quarrel that would gain momentum and extend into the next century. The question was: since New Comedy treats everyday situations and embraces low characters, should it retain conventions of language from Roman comedy or would prose be a more suitable vehicle? The early Italian translations of Latin comedy had set a precedent by their reliance on metrical, if labored, lines. Most critics like Daniello (1536), Giraldi Cintio (1554), Giason de Nores (1587), and Faustino Summo (1592) argued strongly for verse, lumping together tragedy and comedy, since in classical theater they were distinguished in part by reliance on different meters.[7] Others like Giovanni Pigna (1545), Alessandro Piccolomini (1575), and Agostino Richele (1592) allowed comedy in prose. The proportional split in these opinions accurately reflects the choices made by such men as Aretino, who preferred prose, and Alamanni and Dolce, who tended to support Ariosto's solution.

Ariosto had anticipated this contentious discussion and compromised with the so-called *verso sdrucciolo* or *giambi volgari.* This eleven- or twelve-syllable line of verse ending in an unrhymed dactyl (e.g., *L'indústria*) was meant to approximate in the vernacular the clear and direct speech of the sometimes hectic, sometimes crisp, iambic trimeter of Roman comedy, whose lyric portions are extremely fluid and typified by lines of unequal length and frequent changes of metrical pace. It was this verse in which he refashioned *La Cassaria* and *I Suppositi* and in which he wrote all his subsequent comedies. Still, authorized prose versions were published in 1524 and 1525. Especially in the case of the *Cassaria*, besides the modernizing of its locale, changes in the design of language extended to the reshaping of character roles. A new view of the exchange quoted earlier between Trappola and Lucrano (now named Lucramo) reveals a less caricatural and more controlled characterization, in addition to the suppression of satire on Roman ways.

LUCRAMO: È ruffiano
TRAPPOLA: L'industria
      mia principal.
TRAPPOLA: Riportator, maledico,
      seminator di discordie e di scandali.
LUCRAMO: Non ti affaticar più: senza alcun dubbio
      tu di me cerchi. Ricordare il proprio
      mio nome ti voglio anco: ho nome Lucramo.
TRAPPOLA: Lucramo col malanno.
LUCRAMO: A te sol.
TRAPPOLA: Lucramo
      cerco appunto.
LUCRAMO: Io son quel che cerchi. Or narrami:
      che vòi da me?

The *verso sdrucciolo* did not earn Ariosto the acclaim he had hoped for. His disappointment shows through his response to a letter of Federico Gonzaga: "It seemed to me they [the comedies in verse] were better than in prose; but opinions vary." [8]

Ariosto's next comedy was written for the Carnival at Rome in 1520, but was first seen some ten years later. Like the Ferrara of *I Suppositi*, the Cremona of *Il Negromante* is the arbitrary setting for the Terentian satire on contemporary manners. Although borrowings from classical comedy are evident in his characterizations, situations, and dialogue, he is as concerned here as in *I Suppositi* to update them and to play off inhabitants of one regional province or city against those of its competitor. With a conniving glance at Leo X, his original prologue implies that the crimes of the characters are not so great as to have to pay the high price of a plenary indulgence. Indeed, they are merely venial.

Rich like the typical Ariostan father, Massimo plans to marry his adopted son Cintio to Emilia, the daughter of his old and good friend Abbondio. But, also typically Ariostan, Massimo is momentarily out of touch with his son, who already has secretly married Lavinia, the daughter (?) of the amenable Fazio, who is of slightly lower social standing. Rushed into his second marriage, Cintio pretends impotence in order to have the marriage annulled before consummation and so remain faithful to Lavinia. Thus, he contributes to a progressive elevation in feeling on the part of the hero-in-love that was absent in *La Cassaria* but began to appear in *I Suppositi*. At this point, his father brings on the play's archvillain, the magician Iachelino, who will purportedly attempt to cure Cintio but in reality sets out to fleece everyone—except for the astute servant Temolo, whose common sense proves to be more than a match for him. Fazio tries to outbid Massimo for the magician's services, and thus have the second marriage annulled, while Camillo, a parody of the Petrarchan lover, tries to win Emilia by magic art. The expected recognition is prepared when the witless Camillo is persuaded by Iachelino to enclose himself in a trunk (all the better to be robbed) and thus happens to overhear a conversation between Cintio and Lavinia, revealing their marriage. When Massimo learns of the first marriage, he also learns that Lavinia is really his daughter who was born and separated from him during the Venetian occupation of Cremona. Annullment of the second marriage removes the last obstacle to the marriage of the adopted son and legitimate daughter. Emilia and Camillo will also marry.

Meanwhile, Iachelino escapes, but remains the most enduring figure in the play. His character traits resemble those of Rulfo in Bibbiena's *Calandria*.[9] He springs, however, from the traditional line of mystifiers that goes back to classical antiquity and which in the Renaissance assumed the guise of the magus astrologer, alchemist, and dabbler in other occult arts, both black and white. Humanist philosophers had rejected the religious notions of punishment for sin, but they believed in magic and in casting out evil spirits, as though in instinctive substitution for the chains thrown off. Such men as Ficino shared these superstitions, and even one of the most independent thinkers of the period, Pico della Mirandola, saw in the magician a man "who unites heaven and earth in marriage, and brings the netherworld into touch with the powers of the world above." [10] This assertion reinforced Pico's belief that man molds his destiny and descends and ascends in the scale of being. As a wandering Jew in exile from Spain but professing various nationalities, Iachelino resembles no one so much as Johannes Reuchlin's Marranus in *De arte cabalistica* (1517). The essential difference is that Iachelino believes in nothing but the larcenous motives and self-interest of men, and so becomes the negative reference point in the play for the triumph of hope.

Ferrara is again the scene for Ariosto's last completed comedy, *La Lena*, as was appropriate for the wedding celebration of Ercole II and Renée de France at which it was performed in December of 1528. As usual, the play actually premiered at the Carnival of that year. In the preface the "author" addresses a festive audience and speaks of putting on his mask. He alludes ironically to the sixteen masked actors and himself who will have the temerity to rival the ancients. This rivalry is achieved by being at once less dependent on Roman comedy for its stock materials and more satirical. Gone are the corps of superior servants who catalyze the drama, though Corbolo actually claims a lineage with the witty Roman servant, and gone is the miraculous discovery of a son or daughter, presumed lost. Ariosto has completely redone and darkened the good and stolid burgher Fazio from the *Negromante*, who is now made to keep both his lover Lena and her opportunistic husband Pacifico, but hardly in grand style. Though now base in character, Fazio has retained his bourgeois pretensions. His desire for Lena allows him to tolerate the many lovers she has had, but his patience is strained by the procuring she has taken on in her twilight years, especially when this involves his own daughter Licinia, whose domestic talents Lena was supposed to oversee. For the price of twenty-five florins Lena has contracted with Flavio to deliver Licinia to a rendezvous. When a surveyor unexpectedly shows up at the same sight, Flavio is frightened into hiding in a barrel. Through a chance occurrence, the barrel ends up at Fazio's house and Flavio ends up in bed with Licinia. When the lovers are discovered by a servant, Flavio's father arranges a speedy marriage. In the end Lena goes back to Fazio.

La Lena occupies a peculiar place among Ariosto's comedies. Critical opinion, both in his time and in ours, has considered it one of the best plays of the period, alongside the reworked *Cassaria*; but critics have not much known what to do with *Lena* because of the way in which Roman comedy has there become a more serious social drama, treating money as an economic factor that shapes lives. Ferrara is now a specific, not a conventional, setting, and the corruption of its citizens extends from the *contadino* to the usurer to the *Podestà* and even to Duke Ercole as the embodiment of the government. In this measure, Ariosto seems to depart from the atopical and apolitical thematics of New Comedy. Aside from Flavio and Licinia, who simply seek and find one another, Fazio, Pacifico, and Lena are not without a complex vision of things which enables them briefly to glimpse the self-defeating circle that encloses their lives.

In his last comedy, *Gli Studenti*, Ariosto himself returned to the situation intrigue that had obtained in his first efforts, but with more complications. It is likely, in fact, that he began outlining the play before the first performance of *Il Negromante*. He did not complete it, however, and the versions left to us that were finished by Virginio and Gabriele Ariosti are called, respectively, *L'Imperfetta* and *La Scolastica*. Until the last sixty years, the latter version was thought to be entirely by Ariosto's hand.

Again we have two student lovers—Eurialo, who loves the servant girl Ippolita, and Claudio, who loves none other than Flamminia, the daughter of Professor Lazzaro with whom the boys lodge in Pavia. Naturally, the professor discovers the intrigue and chases Claudio from the city, while Eurialo is summoned back to his native Ferrara by his father Bartolo. Due to the political maelstrom in Northern Italy, Lazzaro leaves Pavia and heads for Ferrara to visit his friend Bartolo. He is preceded by Ippolita and a friend whom Eurialo takes into his house, masquerading them as Signora Lazzaro and daughter. All parties converge as the insanely jealous Claudio suspects his friend of duplicity, and Bartolo returns to Ferrara to greet his old friend.

Comparison of textual evidence indicates that Ariosto never went beyond having a servant arrange for a substitute Bartolo to intercept Lazzaro. Virginio and Gabriele bring together loose ends by the usual conciliation—Lazzaro with Claudio, who marries Flamminia—and a discovery—that Ippolita is really an old friend's daughter to whom he delivers a dowry for her marriage with Eurialo. Bald narration of the plot situation is intricate, whereas the plot action is relatively simple. Flamminia never actually appears on stage, and the cleric who absolves Bartolo for misusing his friend's money is instrumental only for the continuing satirical thrust at the abuse of indulgences. Except for the strong reliance on "double action" which was then growing in critical favor, *Gli Studenti* relies less on classical material than any of Ariosto's other plays. Satire is not as pointed as it was in *La Lena*, yet the author's conscience is just as atuned to social and political injustice and to the rich comic substance latent in clerical abuse and Roman *dolce vita*. Scenes are habitually crosshatched by references to events in and around Ariosto's life.

I   *The Mirror of Satire*

The comic typecasting which Ariosto drew from the contemporary scene and filtered through his literary memory and satiric imagination was close to his basic urge to write satire as a genre per se and was coterminal with its composition. On the surface, his seven satires written in *terza rima* appear to be his most autobiographical works. Despite their salutations to specific intended recipients and their occasionally confessional tone, we must be circumspect in imputing attitudes to their author and in accepting his self-judgments at face value. His sustained laments over the contrary tugs of having to curry favor with his Este patrons while desiring to lead a contemplative life, and his grief at having wasted his youth in fruitless studies (*Satire* VI, 154–59), do correspond with what we know of the prosaic life he led. Yet much of what we think we know about Ariosto's life is what we have gleaned from these satires, and these last two complaints, among others, also happen to correspond with literary themes on which lyric poets had for centuries enjoyed embroidering variations.[11] As he admitted in the prologues to his New Comedies, Ariosto is clearly trying to rival classical literature on its own ground, and as his guide and model for satire he elects Horace.

This very choice signaled a turning away from the common trend of satiric invective, not unlike the turn of New Comedy away from the Old. Following Aristotle in the *Ethics*, Horace had prescribed the Golden Mean as the reference point for virtue in all things, including satire, and placed it apart from the excessive vitriol and inappropriate laughter of the buffoon.[12] In the generation before Ariosto the practical jokes of Gonnella, the court fool of the Este entourage, had been enjoyed by malicious minds simply for the spectacle he offered, but had been suffered in silence by the victims. At her death, Beatrice d'Este's favorite fool, Frittalla, took advantage of the occasion and his license as a comedian and buffoon to claim that "the vicious wildcat" would be mourned by few. Medici taste reflected the Florentine cultivation of professional jesters, and none more than Leo X and his surrogate Bibbiena shared in this enjoyment. The tradition of the sharp and outlandish tongue was followed up during Ariosto's time by Francesco Berni and above all by the "incomparable" Aretino, whose misanthropy and sacrifice of scruple to effect were summed up totally in his byword "Veritas odium parit" ("The Truth produces hatred"). It was against this acrimony and against Aretino in particular that Ariosto set off his preferred models "Terenzio, . . . Orazio e le plautine / scene" (*Sat.* V, 96, 143). Beyond being a literary credo, his preference for satire as a "mirror of daily life"[13] and for a mood of reserve and freedom reflect a whole view of life shaded by moderation, perhaps even resignation. The Horatian calm shines through the very incipit of the 1502 *Epithalamium* to Lucrezia Borgia, "Omnia vertuntur" ("All things change").[14] Later we will see that the theme of man's eternal dissatisfaction with his limits, dressed up in the myth of the ascent of Mount Fortune in quest of the moon (*Sat.* III), is a central motif in the *Furioso.*

The *Satire* did not appear in print until almost a year after Ariosto's death, and the subsequent editions leading up to the first authorized publication by the reliable Gabriel Giolito in 1550 were fragmentary, suspicious, and penultimate at best.[15] As a result, the precise chronological ordering according to the date of composition and the author's intent remain speculative. Still, it is possible to establish a sequential order in which allusions to specific events and personalities follow the successive phases of his life. The first satire, dedicated—more than dispatched—to his brother Alessandro and Ludovico da Bagno (ca. October, 1517), follows upon and was occasioned by his break with Ippolito in the unpleasant aftermath of having refused to accompany the cardinal to Hungary. As a righteous and outspoken rejoinder of a subaltern to a superior who has wronged him, it is a fitting and significant prolegomenon to a collection of satires—for one of the deep roots of satire is the wish to restore balance in a world gone mad or beyond caring, a wish based on the assumption that the poet's status as a shunted outsider affords him a distanced perspective against which he can judge the world, while his hurt pride affords him the motive to do so. The narrative line of this declaration of independence threads imperceptibly between the wandering of the poet's imagination and its context of harsh reality. The thought of the Este court in Budapest leads him to apostrophize and call to account Ruggiero, the bumbling hero of the *Furioso* and mythical progenitor of the Este line. A vague familial reference to Naples, where his brother Carlo has established business interests, leads to the paraphrase "where the Turks pursued my Cleandro" (v. 200), a more precise reference to the action of *I Suppositi*. Establishment of local color through reference to fictional analogues indicates that the concept of the *Satire* as a literary exemplar was foremost in Ariosto's mind. When his invocation to the titular god of poetry—"Apollo, have mercy, have mercy, sacred assembly of the Muses, I have not received enough from you to make myself a coat" (vv. 88–90) —attributes his wretched state to the insensitive cardinal, we are reminded that, according to Horace, men who are unregenerate sinners will naturally abhor the satirist's sting and fail to appreciate the poet's gift.[16]

The first satire initiated the themes that will be developed by those that follow. Aside from the early allusion to Ixion's wheel, emblematic of eternal dissatisfaction, the second satire, to his brother Galasso (ca. December, 1517), is mainly concerned with evoking through its savage indignation the curial degeneracy he would find in Rome, the intrigue, and the abuses of nepotism, just as his comedies had attacked abusive sale of indulgences. In the next one (March, 1518), to his cousin Annibale Malaguzzi, the satirist steps back to consider the ambitions that drive men to pursue vain, illusory, or impossible goals. His preference for travelling through the world by following the legend of a map is in effect an apology *pro domo suo*. But the reference to his own submissive audience with the Pope in no way excludes him from the common run of men.[17]

The attraction of his native Ferrara is a motif that bridges the five intervening years before the next satire (February, 1523), written to Sigismondo Malaguzzi. Giving us to understand that he is writing from exile in the Garfagnana, the author leavens his poem with a substantial amount of melancholy, which until that point had been only implicit in the satires. Despite his assertion that he has been forsaken by Apollo, silenced like a bird in a cage, the deeply etched memory of his beloved Alessandra and of the tranquil life he would like to lead with her far from the barbarism of the hill people inspires a mountainscape of eloquent emptiness and silence: "This is a deep gorge I inhabit, where I take no step without climbing the proud slope of the wooded Apennines" (vv. 142–44).

From this dulcit melancholy there is an abrupt transition to the saline barbs of presumably the next satire. Again the poet addressed Annibale Malaguzzi, this time on the occasion of his marriage to Lucrezia Pio.[18] This is the only time when Ariosto seems to leave Horace and follow the Juvenal of the famous sixth satire against women; but the diatribe against marriage and clerical celibacy, and the notion that the best assurances of conjugal fidelity are a keen eye and a suspicious mind, could all have come from Boccaccio. Serialized as either the sixth or seventh satire is the letter (ca. April, 1524) to Bonaventura Pistofilo, who had recommended Ariosto for an ambassadorship to the court of Clement VII. It rhapsodizes the reasons (again, his studies and Alessandra) why he must refuse the assignment. Numerous memories of his sad experiences at the court of Leo X punctuate the letter and show us why he has no wish to return to Rome, even if it does mean escaping from exile in Garfagnana. Through the moralistic fable of the shallow-rooted pumpkin that displaced the firmly rooted pear tree, Ariosto conveys his disbelief at having been displaced at court by superficial courtiers. Yet the legendary Roman geography laid out at the end of the poem is more than antiquarian show, and the list of poets and humanists—Bembo, Sadoleto, Molza, Vida, Tebaldeo—is more than a contemporary who's who; it is another of the compelling reasons why Rome continued to claim the allegiance of educated men no matter how great their disgust at the city's present corruption.

By far the best known of Ariosto's satires is the seventh (or sixth), a compendium in miniature of the vices and virtues of Renaissance humanism, composed between 1524 and 1525. The setting of the epistle to Bembo is again the Garfagnana, where Virginio Ariosto had accompanied his father. The time has come, says the solicitous father, to oversee his son's education, and who better to find a tutor than the illustrious Bembo? It was under Bembo's guidance, after all, that Ariosto rid the second edition of the *Furioso* of dialectical impurities and substituted the more appropriate *lingua toscana*. Ludovico's request that Bembo seek "some good Greek" in Padua or Venice recalls not only his own fond wish to have mastered both classical languages, but also the Turkish conquest of Constantinople, which caused many Greek scholars to flee to the Republic of Venice, where they helped to spread enthusiasm for the Greek classics. But this request immediately gives way to a sovereign contempt for all humanist scholars who fail to temper their vast knowledge with a moral conscience; this caution was to become an instinctive commonplace among sixteenth-century humanists concerned with education. The scope of his diatribe encompasses small vices like the humanist mania for classicizing common names and the presumptuous inquiries of the likes of Luther into the will of God. To the pretentious undertaking and mythological lore of his contemporaries Ariosto contrasts the simple theogonies and manners of Arcadian times, just as he prefers a more modulated reproach to the ad hominem invective of Pistoia and Aretino. Horatian generalities, and indeed all of classical letters that are unsullied by the glossing of humanists, teach man more about humanity.

To convey this learning, Ariosto wants to find for Virginio a preceptor as wise and humane as his own Gregorio da Spoleto. These invitations to the contemplative life are broken by reflections on his active life, but the digressions are not malapropos; he hopes that Virginio will have the leisure to pursue and crown the study of humanities which he himself was forced by family responsibilities to abandon. No Pico della Mirandola, his dilemma is admirably summed up with sad humor: "From a poet he [Ippolito] made me into a postman.[19] Over the cliffs and ditches just imagine how I could have learned Greek or Chaldean."

Again, however, we must recall that the opposition of contemplative life to the active life was a common theme in expository writing and even in school exercises. We can well imagine that before Bembo would have picked up on any newsy information about Ariosto's life from these antithetical themes, he would have applauded their observance of form and method. A letter Ariosto wrote to him in February, 1531, would have enabled Cardinal Bembo to appreciate even more the sharp difference between the 247 line literary exercise we have just seen and a prosaic news item of slightly more than one hundred words in which Ludovico reports in almost telegraphic style: "My son Virginio is going to Padova to study . . . I ask Your Excellence to help him wherever he has need, and whenever you see him to admonish and exhort him not to waste time." [20]

The blunt contrast of these two letters points up the overlay of artfulness on autobiography in the *Satire* which Ariosto's casual style disguises to the point of imperceptibility. Yet nothing is more characteristic of the consciously Horatian satirist than this studied casualness. Since the *sermones* address common humanity in routine situations, Horace insisted that they be written in a plain, discursive style; at the same time, he realized that an unadorned appearance is a difficult illusion to maintain and a deceptively arduous mode to imitate.[21] Intrinsic to this ordinary approach is the notion of *satura lanx*, or full medley of stylistic modulations, which vary according to the rapid shifts that accompany normal conversation and hide the fundamental unity of the satire. Ariosto uses every narrative device at his command—asides, apostrophes to the gods, seeming digressions, and literary sighs—but always with a sense of efficiency: nothing is done without a purpose. Mimesis is involved, but the generic end is rhetorical. Adherence to such a scheme and to the typology which Horace had introduced to satire from New Comedy allows Ariosto to inveigh against the frailty of human institutions like marriage, pompous humanism, and the ecclesiastical hierarchy from the lowest cleric to His Holiness, and to do so by occasionally christening his victims with names that etymologically bestow on them a broad humanity and venial attributes. In the second satire, for instance, Ariosto transformed Horace's thief Voranus (*Sat.* I, viii, 39) into the arch-glutton Vorano, whose name dictates his voracious habits and justifies the caricature assigned to him: a greasy-jowled pig with his snout buried in his plate, born into this world only to eliminate the food with which he stuffs himself (vv. 31–33). Vorano is followed on the comic stage of satire by the miniature portrait of Frate Ciurla ("Brother Drunkard"). Thus, while satire in Aretino and Pistoia tended to shrivel into personal lampoon or oratory, it survived in Ariosto through the agency of its Horatian fictions. His satire compromises between creating something new and exposing the real evil in the existing, between detecting an evil and projecting a hypothetical image of its potential. In his satires Ariosto attacked the personified causes of his chagrin and laid bare a poeticized reality that he celebrated in his epideictic and lyric verse.

II *The Lyric Voice*

In January of 1532, Ariosto wrote to the Duke of Mantua about some "cosette" ("little things") he was planning to publish. The nondescript label was appropriate for a heterogeneous collection of lyric and occasional poems that he was never able to winnow and order definitively during his lifetime. The first of twenty-five posthumous publications in the sixteenth century was the 1546 edition of sixty-four sonnets, madrigals, canzoni, stanzas, and *capitoli* (elegies); the first publication of his Latin works, which did not appear until Pigna edited and unfortunately "corrected" them in 1553, was fifty-four poems that had filtered through the hands of Virginio Ariosto. In all, the authenticated corpus of these poems now extends to five canzoni, forty-one sonnets, twelve madrigals, twenty-seven *capitoli*, two eclogues, eleven stanzas, and seventy-one Latin pieces. As with other seminal writers who were preoccupied with a magnum opus but showed small concern for enshrining their subsidiary works, the apocryphal poems ascribed to Ariosto are half again as numerous as the genuine.[22]

Except for desultory returns to his minor verse that straggled on until his death, the bulk of his Latin and Italian poems were written between the tutelage under Gregorio da Spoleto and the beginning of his service to Ippolito d'Este, that is to say, during the midsection of his life. This historical fact is at the same time a comment of literary significance, because the interest of this poetry consists partially in the tradition it derives from and the mature works of Ariosto it points to. Behind many of the lyrics in both languages that were written to commemorate or castigate specific occurrences, the reader discerns the Latin models which the enthusiastic schoolboy imitated under his master's eye, "meum Gregorium" as he puts it (cf. *Lyrica latina* VII). Prosopopoeic Italian poems in which he fulfilled his obligation as a courtier exercised his ability to write at different levels of style, as when he spoke through the mouth of Melibeo in Eclogue I on the conspiracy of Don Giulio d'Este or wrote beyond the grave from Filiberta of Savoy to Giuliano de' Medici and replied in his behalf (*Canzoni* IV and V). Other individual pieces smack of assigned school exercises, like "De laudibus philosophiae" (I), in which the aspiring poet imagines a counsel of legendary gods who presided at the birth of art, science, and law. We can readily appreciate why Carducci held that Ariosto's early intellectual formation was entirely Latin and even why Bembo attempted to sway him toward writing his masterpiece in the language of Vergil. In the elegiac form of Tibullus, "Ad Pandulphum" (III) laments the invasion of Louis XII at the behest of Alexander VI, and the Horatian calm in the perfect four foot, four verse, four stanza alcaic ode "Ad Philiroëm" (II) supports the contention of the shepherd protagonist that the background rumor and noise of the invasion of Charles VIII will not disturb his pastoral love. Although the Italian sonnets are sprinkled with one-line fragments of Classical Latin poets and are interspersed with pieces that might eventually have been excluded,[23] Alessandra figures occasionally among the themes and execution that unfailingly recall the Petrarchan sonnet sequence. After the initial sonnet and canzone honoring the fatal meeting with the lodestar of his desire, the arrangement of the subsequent episodes hardly matters. The point is that the constant lover relays to his prospective reader the requisite episodic stages of amatory and quasi-religious emotion that he "feels": he hopes and despairs in his prison of love, revisits the site of his capture, sings of her eyes that make the sun pale, weeps over a lock of her hair, and debates the respective value of her beauty and mind, of her beauty and his faith, and so on.[24] To this extent, the sonnets do not essentially differ from the academic exercises in which schoolboys were made to portray a succession of conflicting emotions in literary forms that had been sanctioned by tradition. Other groups of poems restate Petrarchan themes, such as the emotions of love that surpass the storm he weathers at sea [25] and the civil war of conflicting feelings, yet without the affective continuity and serialized drama of the sonnet chain.

Ariosto's classical formation and his flirtation with Petrarchism were undoubtedly instrumental in distilling the sense of meter and in building the command of language with which the *Furioso* is credited. The lateral reference in the *Satire* to other more acclaimed genres he was polishing at the time recurs in the later Latin poems. The acerb "In Lenam" (XXI) with its "venditrix libidinum" calls to mind the hapless protagonist of *La Lena*, but without the indulgence of the comic dramatist. More significantly, "De Eulalia" (XXIX) is a paradigm of Renaissance *contaminatio* —the blending of disparate sources to form an original fiction. It begins by celebrating "Eulalia, hispanae filia Pasiphiles" ("Eulalia, the daughter of Spanish Pasiphilo") and ends by warning her that whenever old age sneaks up on her, unable to live by prostitution, she can become a procuress (*lena*). Thus, Plautus and Terence are obliquely combined and transformed, as Ariosto brings together characters and character attributes from the *Cassaria, Suppositi,* and *Lena.* Transferal of stereotyped passages from one text to another with appropriate modifications was a license that poets allowed themselves in dispatching similar love poems to various mistresses merely by altering a proper name. In those cases where we have princeps and modified versions of both Latin and Italian poems, we learn something about the stratified stages of composition. The alternate version of the ode "Ad Philiroëm" resembles the final version, from the opening invocation to "Galliarum rex Carolus," until the apostrophe "O miseri" directed to the insane minds who sell their blood for gold (vv. 9–33); it is the rejected version, however, that we find in the *Cinque Canti,* from the passage on "La mercenaria mal fida canaglia" up to the new section that begins "Carlo per tutta Francia e per la Magna" (II, 43–45).

The most significant instance of cross-fertilization and of the community of literary models in which Ariosto moved is the passage that ends up in *Orlando Furioso*, XLIV, 61–65, where Bradamante makes Ruggiero aware of her enduring faith. The passage is introduced by the statement "gli fe queste parole un dí sapere" ("one day she let him know these words"), which coyly avoids saying that she actually said them or felt them in her heart. Ruggiero could have read them just as easily in *Capitoli* XIII (if we can overlook the anachronism), where the essence of the whole passage appears, somewhat rearranged and minus any mention of his name. But then he could also have read the keynote line "qual sempre fui, tal esser voglio fin alla morte" ("what I have been I wish to be until death") in a sonnet of Ariosto's acquaintance Tebaldeo, in his model, Boiardo, or in their own source, Petrarch.[26] Or even in the original locus of the idea, the conclusion to one of Horace's odes (I, xxii, 17–24). Horace would be the most distant source in time and in terms of his imagery and likely impact in this instance. But the Latinate syntax of the *capitolo* is more suggestively Horatian than that of Bradamante's message.

che d'ogni intorno il vento e il mar percuote:
ch'l vento indarno, indarno il
. . . luogo mutai, né muterò in eterno.   [flusso alterno.[27]

If Latin rhetoric whetted his youthful enthusiasm, it was ultimately an interval he was to transcend on the way to his uniquely personal *vulgari eloquentia*.

III *Aftermath*

As laudable as Ariosto's comedies, satires, and much of his miscellaneous poetry undoubtedly are, they do not begin to approach the stupendous impact of the *Furioso* on European literature of the sixteenth and seventeenth centuries. Any real influence the *Satire* may have exerted on subsequent developments of the genre is imperceptible, if it existed at all, mainly because Ariosto operated confortably within the Horatian tradition without substantially altering it. The first English translation of the seven letters by Robert Tofte in 1608 [28] actually mistranslated some passages by inserting Horatian turns of phrase that the original text did not authorize. Even more significant, the autobiographical element was blurred in favor of a more universalized relevance (e.g., *Sat*. II: "Of Libertie, and the Clergie in generall"; *Sat*. VII: "Of Honour, and the happiest Life") more in keeping with the developing nature of the Renaissance essay. Near the end of the sixteenth century in France, Jean de la Taille paid Ariosto the signal honor of dispensing with his name, equating the "lyrique romain" with "le Ferrarois." He went on to translate six satires, adapting to the French scene the personages under attack in the Italian courts. But as Alexandre Cioranescu rightly pointed out, Ariosto's introspective mood was not congenial with the militant demands of satire during the Counter Reformation.[29]

The Italian lyrics fared better in posterity, especially the sonnets. In Golden Age Spain evidence of a readership, let alone any influence, is meager.[30] While only Du Bellay and his shadow Olivier de Magny seem to have read the *Satire*, the Pléiade poets raised Ariosto to a level among nonclassical writers that was surpassed only by Petrarch. Except for the relatively ephemeral efforts of Baïf to incorporate Ariostan syntactic and versifying skill, the youthful group saw Ariosto's poems as a thesaurus from which to glean images of delicate contour or erotic force.[31] Their favorites were the eighth *capitolo*, with its relating of a night of lovemaking, and the ninth, in which suspicious eyes and loose tongues become obstacles to the narrator's sensual gratification. Among the sonnets, the following were the most popular: the ninth, with its farfetched conceit dramatizing the beloved's hair, a golden net that ensnares him, and her eyes and brows, the bows and glances that transfix him; the twentieth, that compares the force of nature to the violence of love; and the twenty-fifth, in which her beauty is surpassed only by his faith. Across the Channel it was this last sonnet, "Madonna sete bella e bella tanto," that Thomas Lodge paraphrased in the anthology piece that made his fame, "Faire art thou, Phillis, ay so faire."

Beyond comparison with any of his other minor works, it was Ariosto's theater that commanded the greatest esteem in Europe. The very editions of the *Cassaria* and *Suppositi* that he denounced as bastardized suggest the extent to which he was lionized as the epitome of regular drama; correspondingly, his fall from grace during the Romantic period derived precisely from the high classical values he exemplified. The appearance of Ariosto's theater in France occurred with the now lost translation of *I Suppositi* by Jacques Bourgeois.[32] This translation was followed by the bilingual version of Jean-Pierre de Mesmes, who may have been instrumental in introducing Ariosto to the Pléiade. Subsequent borrowings from the play were altered for French consumption; *Les Déguisés* of Jean Godard (1590) gallicizes both characters and locales, and traces of *I Suppositi* in Jean de la Taille's *Les Corrivaux* (ca. 1560) are so scant as to be conjectural. La Taille's translation (ca. 1550) of *Il Negromante* and that of Juan de Timoneda in his Spanish comedy *Cornelia* (1559) range between faithful translation and paraphrase that was free enough to accommodate the times and customs of other societies. Ariosto's flair for fast-paced dialogue led Rotrou in *Les Sosies* (I, ii; IV, i–ii) and Molière in *Amphitryon* (I, ii; III, ii) to adapt sections of verse in scene changes and in altercations between servant and master. It was in Elizabethan England that the survival of Ariosto's influence passed beyond the footnotes of literary histories. The 1566 translation of George Gascoigne gave *I Suppositi* the unique distinction of being the first Italian comedy to be translated into English and also of being the first English play to use prose dialogue. The evident fact that Gascoigne worked simultaneously or at least successively from both the verse and prose texts suggests that both may have circulated widely. In any event, they circulated widely enough to have served Spenser as a model for his nine lost comeries. Through the intermediary of Gascoigne's *Supposes, I Suppositi* furnished the subplot for *Taming of the Shrew* dealing with Bianca and her lovers.[33] The exchange between Biondello, the servant of Lucentio, and Bianca, the very ploy of gaining access to Bianca in the guise of a tutor, and the pretense of political danger by which the pedant is induced to play his part are all patently Ariostan.

Taken together these adaptations and others like them are numerous and appear in a spate of different circumstances—as imagery, dialogue, situation, social commentary. But individually none of them can be said to have redirected a writer's literary experience or to have contributed to his mature creative vision.

Their high incidence and broad application are essentially derivative in popularity because, as would have been the case with any other work Ariosto could have written, they are necessarily satellites to the *Orlando Furioso*.

CHAPTER 3

Oh, Great Goodness of the Ancient Knights

(*Orlando Furioso*, I, 22)

WITH his characteristic gift for generalization, C. S. Lewis defined the perspective on reality in the Italian epic: "In the foreground we have fantastic adventure, in the middle distance daily life, in the background a venerable legend with a core of momentous historical truth." [1] The distant historical truth for the Italian poems was the defeat of the forces of Charlemagne at the hands of Basque rebels in 778; the dimension of legend refers to the heroic exaggeration of the event in the *chansons de geste*, which lent tragic overtones to the military skirmish and transformed border rebels into Saracens and other congenital enemies of Western Christianity. The heroes were feudal barons, and the virtues which the *chansons* extolled were the courage, fidelity, and piety of Roland, just as they anathematized the treachery of Ganelon. An even more prominent source of heroic legend was the medieval romances that leavened the ethos of the *chanson de geste* with Arthurian mythology and with other concerns that made war a metaphor for love. The three main branches of this genre are: romances of antiquity, such as a poeticized life of Alexander the Great, the legend of Thebes, a retelling of the story of Aeneas and the story of the sack of Troy; Breton romances deriving from the *matière de Bretagne*, dealing with the court of King Arthur and highlighted by the novels of Chrétien de Troyes that analyzed the crises of conscience in a superannuated knighthood; and the romances of adventure drawn from the three cycles of the *chansons de geste*. Although the *chansons de geste* and the early French romances are both poetic narratives, the romances have even less historical basis than the *chansons* have, and evince a greater concern for artistic embellishment, by replacing assonance with verse, and for refined analysis of character, and have a greater proportion of magical or marvelous deeds that go beyond even the fantastic feats of prowess in the *chansons*.

Above all, the medieval romance is more motivated by the passions of the heart. Of the 4,002 verses in the *Chanson de Roland*, only a handful speak of "la belle Aude," whereas with Chrétien, aside from the special case of *Li Contes del Graal*, all his romances integrate the motif of love into the problems of chivalry. This change occurred during the course of the twelfth century, when feudal civilization purified and cultivated itself. The life of the court, much like that in the various Italian Renaissance courts with their refined and conventional manners, was exactly described as "courteous." It was first developed, not in the entourage of the king, who long continued faithful to the Carolingian tradition, but in princely residences. It was there that the rules and the ceremonial of chivalry were established; there that the worship of womanhood first made its appearance.

The Roland legend reached into all corners of Europe, and it appeared in the East wherever the Christians had established themselves, because French was the language spoken in Jerusalem, Antioch, and Saint-Jean d'Acre. Roland was the ideal knight as imagined by the sons of those who had fought in the First Crusade. Konrad's *Ruolandes Liet* dates from the middle of the twelfth century, the Norwegian prose translation *Karlomagnasaga* followed less than a century later, and in Spain it was grist for popular lore, with the new twist that had the Spanish and the Saracens routing the French. It was in Northern Italy that the "matters" enjoyed the greatest popularity, mostly in Tuscany and Lombardy, although their cultural penetration was universally felt. Rough half-reliefs of Roland and Oliver are found on the portal (1135) of the Verona Cathedral, and a mosaic in the Cathedral of Brindisi (1178) relates various scenes from the *Chanson de Roland*. Over three centuries later at the wedding celebration of Beatrice d'Este (1491), her sister Isabella and Galeazzo Visconti engaged in a passionate discussion over the relative merits of those two famous knights of romance, Rinaldo and Orlando; the last word of the margravine of Mantua on her departure was a cry of "Rinaldo," to which the Milanese courtier shouted that Orlando was the only true hero. The popular appeal of these legends points to sources of transmission that compromise somewhere between aristocratic literature and oral tradition.

Around 1350 a Paduan author writing in a French-inflected dialect penned the *Entrée en Espagne,* in which we see an aged and querulous Charles before the disaster at Roncesvalles. He breaks off his narrative with Roland, now a well-heeled ladies' man, who goes to the Orient to enhance his renown as a warrior. The story harks back to the twelfth-century *Pèlerinage de Charlemagne,* where the Emperor became a fool and his paladins laid aside their mystical élan while they told erotic tales. At the same time, it looks forward to Count Astolfo of the *Furioso,* whose broad outline is apparent in the derisive laughter and derided actions of Estout de Langres. This laughter embracing participant and spectators was also heard on a popular level in Italy. Wandering minstrels accompanying pilgrims and crusaders to the Holy Land had helped to perpetuate the hand-me-down narrative of the older poems and to spread the fame of ancient heroes, Arthur's knights, and their Saracen enemies. In the fifteenth century their stories blended with historical, biblical, and legendary matter to become the stock repertoire of the *cantastorie.* Before small gatherings in a town piazza or before the banquet table of a powerful lord these professional storytellers sang of Carlo and Uliviere, of the bad feelings between the House of Clermont and its champion Orlando on the one hand, and on the other the House of Mayence and its Judas-like representative Gano. Association between Cieco da Ferrara (Francesco Bello), author of the *Mambriano* (1509), and the ancient tradition of the blind and footloose bard increased the link in the minds of many between the wandering *cantastorie* and writers of later chivalric narrative. In the *Erbolato,* a comic diatribe ascribed to Ariosto on quack doctors hawking "elixirs of life" to a gullible public, the footfalls of the travelling bards are clearly heard. Four centuries of a heroic legend that had become variously related, widely dispersed, and fantasized beyond its original measure—this was the legacy that was passed on to Luigi Pulci, Matteo Maria Boiardo, and Ariosto.

Pulci, who had a bit of the Estout de Langres in him, wrote twenty-three cantos of *Il Morgante Maggiore (The Greater Morgante)* in *ottava rima* sometime between 1460 and 1470, brought the total to twenty-eight by 1482, and published the completed work in 1483. The first of these three divisions centers on the adventures of Morgante and owes a substantial debt to the late fourteenth-century Italian metrical romance that Pio Rajna called the *Orlando*. Here Pulci retells the quarrel of Orlando with a stubborn Carlo, of his rancor toward his long-standing enemy Gano, and of his self-exile in the East where in one episode, following a route familiar to pilgrims, he meets three giants who are laying siege to a monastery. He quickly dispatches the first two, but spares and converts the third because of the instinctive admiration and sympathy he feels for him. Thus we meet Morgante, who becomes Orlando's faithful companion. Morgante's size justifies his astonishing exploits, as we watch him form a cross with his body to act as a mast and yardarm, wield a tree for a club, rout an entire herd of ferocious pigs, and kill a whale. This last feat proves to be his undoing, for when he goes to retrieve the dead fish, a crab bites him on the toe and he dies in agony. His death casts a pall over the poem that has suddenly shifted from the comic to the tragic mode. The event falls within the Renaissance fascination with strange and illustrious deaths by which man is moved to respect and marvel at the caprice of Fortune. Morgante's death contrasts with that of his boon companion, the irreverent Margutte. Margutte is more than twice the size of a man, both in his physical stature and lusty appetites. Among his literary ancestors is the mercurial Sosia of Plautus, and among his most notable descendants number Til Eulenspiegel and Rabelais' Panurge, who also enjoyed bragging about their not-so-merry pranks. Margutte actually laughs himself to pieces when he awakes and sees himself mirrored in the antics of a monkey.

The second division relies principally on the late fourteenth-century *Spagna in Rima*, also written in *ottava rima* and also one of Ariosto's occasional sources (cf. *Orlando Furioso*, XII, 48). *La Spagna* is Pulci's main source for chivalric adventures involving enchantments made and broken, battles with kings and monsters, and the ultimate conversion of the vanquished. Sobered by the death of Morgante, Pulci retraces the events leading up to and following the defeat at Roncesvalles, adhering fairly strictly to the cast of characters in the Carolingian cycle and to the tenor and grand design of the *Chanson de Roland*. A third dimension of the work is the total impact of its combined heroism, frivolity, and philosophical thoughtfulness. Commissioned by Lucrezia Tornabuoni and read aloud to the Medici as its composition progressed, *Morgante* gives us an insight into the taste that pre-

vailed during the enlightened despotism of Lorenzo the Magnifi-
cent. Pulci's shafts of satiric wit and his gift for portraiture that
is at once subtle and outlandish enable him to innovate within
a vast tradition. Perhaps no other chivalric work before Ariosto,
with the exception of Boiardo's poem and the *Roland* itself,
exerted such a profound influence on a posterity that included
Rabelais, Cervantes, Spenser, and even Byron. The many shades
in Pulci's humor, his devils, magicians, and a flying horse that
invites man to rise to an Olympian view of reality will all make
their imprint on the *Furioso*.

Boiardo's muse is as self-willed as Pulci's (whom he may never
have read) or Ariosto's. Lacking the voluble laughter of the
former and the prismatic irony of the latter, his *Orlando innamorato* (*Orlando in Love*) is tied by a seamless bond to the romantic love expressed in his incidental works and to what we
know of the high-minded sentiments of his private utterances.
All is summed up in the personal device he chose for himself,
Vergil's "Amor vincit omnia" ("Love conquers all").[2] Still, the
Count of Scandiano shares a coincidental kinship with Ariosto. He
was the governor of Reggio and Modena, and thus served the
Estensi both in a high official capacity and as a eulogist of their
fictional lineage (*OI*, II, xxv, 42–56). And like Ludovico in love
with Alessandra Strozzi, in his mid-thirties Boiardo formed a
lasting attachment for Antonia Caprara, to whom he dedicated
a long and masterful sonnet sequence, and who, so he claimed,
became the guiding inspiration of the *Innamorato*. The first two
books covering sixty cantos were published in 1483; the third
book barely reached the ninth canto before Boiardo's death in
1494—and before his individual heroes were displaced by the
seventeen thousand archers, crossbowmen, halberdiers, and Swiss
mercenaries of the all-victorious Charles VIII, displaying their
white standards with the lily and crown emblem and the inscrip-
tion "Missus a Deo" ("Sent by God"). In Boiardo's poem it is
love, however, that conquers all, including the starry-eyed hero,
who foresakes Carlo and "Sweet France" for which he had laid
down his life four hundred years earlier. The *Morgante* had
portrayed a Roland "che ismarrito havea il cervello" because of
Ganelon's affront to his honor. Our attention in Boiardo is turned
from Saragosa and Ronceveaux in the West, to the East whose
comforts and luxuries had suggested new standards of living to

earlier travelers. Out of Cathay comes Angelica, whose charms seduce Charlemagne's paladins, from Ra[i]naldo to the decrepit Nano, and drive Orlando mad with desire—with Boiardo's seeming approbation. In keeping with the overall evolution of the Roland story from an originally localized occurrence to globetrotting adventures, Orlando and Ranaldo chase Angelica to China and back. In the Orient we see Agricane laying siege to Albracà, the stronghold of Angelica, and in Africa we see the forces of Agramante prepare for the invasion of France. Comings and goings through fields and dark woods are facilitated by magic fountains that make Ranaldo and Angelica alternately love and hate at odds, and by enchanted swords and rings that change hands. These events are interludes in the main action of the titanic struggle of Charlemagne's forces with the Saracen champions Gradasso, Sacripante, Mandricardo, and Agramante, not to mention sundry magicians and devils—such as Brunello and Malagise—that assist both camps. Paris is under siege by Agramante's army at the point where the poem breaks off.

Francesco Berni found Boiardo's narrative so engrossing but its provincial dialect so crude that he felt obliged in 1541 to bring it into line—and thus flatten its individuality—with his notion of elegant norms of style. Along with many other readers of his generation, Ariosto prized Boiardo's individuality. Time and again he acknowledged the *Innamorato's* genius for interweaving disparate story lines and drew generously on its stock of characters. More than Vergil, Ovid, Statius, and the huge body of medieval romances that preceded and included Pulci, the main blueprint for the literally hundreds of interwoven episodes and occurrences in the *Furioso* is the narrative of Boiardo.

Although numerous, the welter of events in the *Furioso* can be reduced to three related strains. Taking up where the *Innamorato* left off, the principal action of Ariosto's poem is the invasion of Christendom and the siege of Paris by the forces of Agramante of Africa, his cohort Marsilio of Spain, and their peerless warriors Mandricardo, the ferocious and immodest Rodomonte, and, until his conversion and baptism, Ruggiero. The deeper roots are still the animosity between the deceitful Ganelon (variously called Ganelone and Gano for reason of metric needs) of the House of Maganza (Mayence) and the House of Clermont. These struggles alternately dominate the foreground with battle scenes that are larger than life and recede for long periods of silence to a distant background. They extend from before the beginning of the poem until the death of Rodomonte in the last stanza—and even beyond into the *Cinque Canti*, which Ariosto may have intended as an extension of or sequel to his work. Many of the knights who take part in this war have their own private lives and loves, like Zerbino in his devotion to Isabella, which they pursue when not fighting and, supposedly, when we are not watching them.

The initial adventures and second strain of the *Furioso*, then, begin in medias res, and assume that the reader is familiar with the epic pseudo-history that forms the poem's backdrop. They concern the love of Orlando for Angelica and his ensuing jealousy that drives him mad and gives the work its title and one of its main themes. In the first canto Angelica has just fled the camp of Charlemagne, where she was brought by Orlando from Cathay. She is pursued by the Saracen Ferraú and Rinaldo, the former Renaud de Montauban of the Doon de Mayence cycle of the *chansons de geste* in which recalcitrant vassals rebelled against Charles. Combat between Ferraú and Rinaldo allows Angelica to escape, only to be courted by the Circassian Sacripante who is unhorsed by Bradamante, Rinaldo's sister, disguised as a knight. Disappearing only to reappear in the narrative fabric, Angelica is successively captured at sea by the inhabitants of the Isle of Ebuda, who intend to offer her to Proteus, a latter-day Minotaur who dines on female flesh; later, after her rescue from an Orc by Ruggiero, mounted on the Hippogriff and armed with his magic shield, she in turn escapes from him with the aid of a ring that makes its wearer invisible; after being delivered from one peril after another, the chaste Angelica finally falls in love with the lowly soldier Medoro, whom she has nursed to health. During all of the tribulations that beset her from the time of her escape from the Christian camp, Angelica has also been sought by Orlando, for whom, unlike any of Angelica's other suitors, she becomes a graillike object, "angelic" as it were, at once mysterious and unattainable. When he finally persuades himself that she has betrayed his faith, he goes mad with jealousy and rages through the countryside, ravaging man and beast alike. His sanity is eventually restored by the British knight Astolfo, who dominates some of the poem's central episodes and yet often observes its happenings from a philosophically detached point of view. Astolfo had flown to the earthly paradise on the back of a winged ass, the Hippogriff, where he met Saint John the Evangelist, who explained the cause of Orlando's madness and accompanied the knight to the moon in order to retrieve Orlando's wits. (Astolfo's voyage to the moon has frequently been extracted from the text for inclusion in divers anthologies.) Once back on earth, Astolfo and others subdue the wild Orlando, restore his mind, and in the process dispel his illusions about love. His identity must be restored and wisdom must displace folly, for only the real Orlando can kill Agramante and Gradasso on the Isle of Lipadusa (or Lampedusa) and lift the siege of Paris. Astolfo goes on to defeat the Saracens, lays siege to Bizerte, and liberates captive knights.

The third strain of the narrative completes the program of Boiardo by following the doings of Ruggiero and extolling the virtue and courage of his future wife, Bradamante. The pair ultimately learn that from their love will spring the illustrious House of Este. The reunification of the couple is partially achieved by the efforts of the good fairy Melissa, who helps them through their many vicissitudes. Just as the Amazonian Bradamante gradually replaces Angelica as the leading heroine, Ruggiero gradually merits the weighty responsibility thrust on him by fate. He is not always mindful of his pledge to Bradamante, fails to learn much from the account of Astolfo's capture by the enchantress Alcina, and at the outset is protected from battle by his guardian Atlante, who builds a castle of illusion for him, much as Achilles was safeguarded by Thetis. But he goes off to aid the Bulgarians in their fight against the Greek emperor, whose son Leone has been selected by Bradamante's parents as her intended husband. When Ruggiero is captured by the man he had set out to kill, Leone frees him and later relinquishes Bradamante, even though Ruggiero, acting in his new friend's behalf, had defeated his lady in battle as a condition imposed by Charles for receiving her hand. Following this interplay of *virtù* and Fortune, Ruggiero becomes king of the Bulgarians. His last trial in these rites of passage is to meet and defeat Rodomonte, who had challenged him as a *mancator di fé*. This third group of events obviously interested Ariosto most in his capacity as apologist and mythographer of the Estensi.

But he also takes great delight in spinning yarns about stories that are listened to by main characters or in which they actually participate, but which have little or nothing to do with the ongoing wars. The most prominent of these *novelle* are the betrayal of Ginevra by Ariodante, which Rinaldo hears in Scotland (cantos IV–VI); the betrayal of Olimpia by Bireno, which keeps Orlando rapt (IX–XI); the tale of the *ménage à trois* involving Astolfo of Lombardy, Giocondo, and Fiammetta, heard by Rodomonte (XXVIII); Marganorre's cruelty to women, which moves Bradamante and Marfisa (XXXVII); and the story told by the Mantuan knight to Rinaldo about conjugal fidelity (XLII–XLIII).[3] Like the encounter of Ruggiero with Leone, the Olimpia and Marganorre interludes were interjected only in the 1532 edition, which also trifurcated the last canto.

The *Cinque Canti* and other fragments, running to a combined total of some 5,600 lines, represent an altogether different kind of *hors d'oeuvre*. Textual ligatures between the forty-sixth canto and the first new canto suggest that Ariosto may have intended to expand his poem to fifty cantos. The five new sections begin after the death of Agramante, the restoration of Orlando, and the marriage of Bradamante and Ruggiero, who, however, is now somehow dispossessed of his Bulgarian kingdom. Ariosto replays the betrayal at Roncesvalles by Ganelon who, while practically missing in the *Furioso*, here becomes the agent of Alcina's vengeance on the army of Charlemagne (I). Charles fights off an attacking enemy and sends Orlando to Latium (II). A misled Rinaldo revolts against Charles, and Ganelon conspires but is captured by Bradamante. This section might eventually have seen the insertion of a long fragment called "The Shield of Gold," which recounts the jealousy and strife of the paladins over the shield that would be given to the *primus inter pares*. Judging from the shield's Vergilian prophecy of a noble lineage, the fragment may originally have been intended for cantos XXXII–XXXIII (III). Contention over the mysterious shield at the end would form a pendant to the contention over the mysterious Angelica at the outset. Heedless, Ruggiero falls into the sea and is imprisoned by Alcina in the belly of a whale, where he discovers a New World (IV). Finally, Rinaldo and Orlando duel, and Charles falls from a bridge but is saved by his horse at the abrupt end of the fifth canto. The reestablished peace, the marriage of Ruggiero and Bradamante, and the death of Rodomonte, which recalls the death of Turnus at the end of the *Aeneid* and

[57]

thus gives the forty-six cantos of the *Furioso* both a Vergilian and Dantesque circularity, all militate against viewing the *Cinque Canti* as a projected addendum to the *Furioso*.[4]

I *Time Present and Time Past*

That the *Furioso*'s vast field of vision is enclosed by reminiscences of classical and medieval epics is not in itself surprising for various reasons. For one, high Renaissance art and literature in many quarters were resilient enough to accommodate veneration for an integral classical antiquity coexisting with a surviving taste for medieval epic and romance narratives, a resilience that often allowed these two currents to respond as analogies to contemporary political, historical, and cultural events. The possible analogues we have already seen between events in the *Furioso* and the Homeric poems could be multiplied by drawing parallels between the shield of Atlante and that of Perseus, between the Hippogriff and Pegasus, between Orrilo and the Hydra. We could read Ulysses' escape from Polyphemus between the lines of Norandino's escape from the Orco (XVII, 54) and, with some textual solicitation, extend the Homeric conflict between Agamemnon and Achilles over Chryseïs, adumbrated in canto I, into canto XXXVI, 78, where the plotted vengeance of Ruggiero and Marfisa harks back to the plot that Electra hatched with the aid of Orestes. For other reasons, the parentage between Vergil and Dante is obvious, and Ariosto's intellectual formation was such that Vergil came instinctively to the tip of his pen. In a letter to Ludovoco Gonzaga, Ariosto interrupts himself in the midst of recounting a narrow escape from papal forces to interject the words of Aeneas retelling his own flight from Troy (*Aen.* II, 12): "Hor hora che sono uscito de le latebre e de' lustri de le fiere e passato alla conversation de gli homini. De' nostri periculi non posso anchora parlare: *animus meminisse horret, lucutque refugit,* e d'altro lato . . ."[5] A century ago Pio Rajna's *Le fonti dell "Orlando Furioso"* displayed the greatness and the failings of scholarship of that time by an immense catalog of the source material Ariosto drew upon; he concluded that the *Furioso* was a degeneration of medieval romance and implied that Ariosto's originality was inversely proportional to the number of his sources, as though creativity could be quantified. Source-hunting scholars have continued and updated this literary archeology—for instance, by seeing analogies between the episode in the whale's mouth and the comparable passages in more recent works like *Pinocchio*.[6]

There is no room here to review Rajna's findings, to propose some of the many new ones that do remain to be found, or to dispute his conclusions. It is enough to say that some modern critics have meticulously analyzed the nature of Ariosto's debt to classical antiquity, to the Middle Ages, and to his own time, concluding that Ariosto's obvious borrowings were meant to be just that—passing nods to literary figures of his own and of former times—and that countless others throughout the entire work are so transformed and so fractional as to become ingredients of the writer's imagination.[7] Without reminding the reader that Ariosto seems to have had Vergil by his side throughout the composition of the *Furioso*, and without listing the sources that Rajna inevitably missed, it will be more instructive to cite but one example as evidence that contemporary and classical allusions often coalesce and to show Ariosto's gift for ingesting source material.

Canto XXXVII treats the crime and punishment of Marganorre and the institution of laws more favorable to the cause of women. More than by the skill of rhetoric or the force of logic, it is the secretive poisoning of Marganorre's son Tanacro by Drusilla, and the example of her own self-immolation at their wedding altar, that move the listeners in the story to enact social justice. Yet the speech she gives achieves a calculated effect before a capacity crowd—"trasseno a udirlo tutti, uomini e donne" ("men and women all hastened to hear it"). At the high point of her discourse she declaims, "Non potendo come avrei voluto, / io t'ho fatto morir come ho potuto" (stanza 72: "not being able to do as I wished, I have made you die as I could"). The translation offered here does not begin to suggest the crucial axis, so clear in the end rhymes, between aspiration (*voluto*) and achievement (*potuto*). The nearest Renaissance locus of this idea and its context of *sic semper tyrannis* is Machiavelli's *Discorsi*, I, 51, which has to do with feigning necessity in instituting tax laws and begins in terms remarkably similar to Drusilla's speech.[8] Following the murder of his son, Marganorre is whipped into such a rage that he drives the women from the town. For twenty stanzas following Drusilla's speech, up to Marganorre's frightful punishment, Ariosto presses the point that for a long time the people were too frightened to act, and he dresses his comments in

Erasmian adages and universalized observations: "Ma 'l populo facea come i piú fanno, / ch'ubbidiscon piú in odio hanno" ("But the people did as most men do, for they most obey those they hate the most"). Again, the nearest reference for the idea is Machiavelli, where it recurs frequently (cf. *The Prince*, chs. 17 and esp. 19; *Discourses on Titus Livy*, III, 6), but this time it has a much deeper resonance. The maxim of Accius, "Oderint dum metuant" (*Atreus*, v. 168), was a frequent theme of composition in Renaissance coypbooks,[9] and crops up in the *Cinque Canti*, II, 4. While working within a community of presences, both living and dead, Ariosto reshapes a timeworn idea in his own distinctive idiom. Drusilla's speech is relayed by Ullania to the other characters, and from Ariosto to us. Thus "distanced," the jaded observation of a political scientist on tax laws gains for a moment the heroic stature of a moral imperative—representative of the extremes of disillusionment and idealism between which the characters in the *Furioso* find themselves constantly torn.[10]

Other links with the Middle Ages and legendary antiquity, of course, play a more overt and much more important thematic role in the poem, beginning with the dedication to Ippolito in the third stanza of the first canto. Ariosto himself has been accused of playing politics by lauding a man he despised in the privacy of the satires, but the point can easily be overstated. Ariosto, Spenser, Giovanni Giorgini, and others could find sanction in the example of Vergil, if it even occurred to them to do so,[11] who had also let his muse sing under a patronage system. In affiliating Bradamante and Ruggiero with the dukes of Ferrara, Britomart and Artegall with Queen Elizabeth, and in making Ferdinand of Spain the leader of an expedition in *il nuovo mondo*, historical veracity was among the least of their concerns. Still, the question of Ariosto's attitude toward the Este line is an important one because it raises other intriguing questions about the attitude of his age itself toward its medieval past and toward an even more distant golden age.[12] Few motifs summoned the attention of Renaissance naturalists, realists, theologians, poets, and humanists as persistently as the ancient myth of a golden age. Set in an imaginary first age of human innocence, the tutelary dominion of a beneficent Saturn and Astrea, the theme was eternalized in Vergil's fourth eclogue, which promised the return of Saturnian order and utopian justice and which set the pattern for countless variations before and after Ariosto. The nostalgic dream invited princes to become philosophers, to trade war for peace, and to restore a society in which *tuum* and *meum* would be one. Such visions bespeak the intense self-awareness of a disturbed and imbalanced age. In the discovery of new worlds and their exotic trappings that gave rise to inspired visions of earthly paradise, disillusioned observers saw primitive societies in which men resembled animals more than pastoral figures, and which European despots exploited in their hunger for gold and guided by expansionist ambition. Ariosto is at pains to establish connection between the events of present times and the past, at first gingerly venturing a comparison between medieval warfare with the Moors and Alfonso d'Este's victory at Ravenna:

> E se alle antique le moderne cose,
> invitto Alfonso, denno assimigliarsi;
> la gran vittoria, onde alle virtuose
> opere vostre può la gloria darsi,
> di ch'aver sempre lacrimose ciglia
> Ravenna debbe, a queste s'assimiglia
>
> [XIV, 2]

And if modern matters can be compared to ancient ones, unconquered Alfonso, the great victory in which your deeds should be glorified, for which Ravenna should always have a tearful eye, may be compared to these [ancient victories].

Later he boldly compares the failures of the Carthagenian invasions of Rome with the defeat of Ludovico "Il Moro" (XL, 41). Though the conceit may seem bombastic and precious, it might not have so struck its beneficiaries. In an age when every ruler read Machiavelli, or at least acted as if he had, when the Christian commonwealth and feudal particularism had both disappeared, the ease is a bit startling with which Ariosto can speak of Francis I—notwithstanding the alliance of Ferrara with France—as the patronym of his country, symbol of Christian unity, and peer of Julius Caesar and Alexander the Great (XXVI, 43, 47). But the comparison can be explained, if not justified, by the awe bestowed on "les neuf preux"—a fascination that dated from the beginning of the fourteenth century, degenerated in the hands of the *rhétoriqueur* Jean Molinet, who wrote a *neuf preux de la gour-*

mandise, and caught the imagination of an aristocracy at play, donning the togas of antiquity or the knightly armor of the feudal past. Francis I, who occasionally outfitted himself as one of the nine worthies, loved to play on medieval themes and traditions, which were still vital under newer forms. Moreover, sixteenth-century editions of the *Furioso* show its medieval heroes wearing Roman armor. Although equal rights dictated eighteen worthies so as to represent both sexes, the original nine were: Joshua, David, and Judas Maccabaeus; King Arthur, Charlemagne, and Godfrey de Bouillon; Hector, Caesar, and Alexander. In the *Furioso* Francis accompanies only the last two simply because the role of Hector was reserved for Ruggiero.

Historical and mythical dimensions in the *Furioso* are in constant flux, preventing us from establishing a permanent narrative reference point in time. The persona of the author respectfully turns aside to Leo X and wonders why men have lost their crusading zeal (XVII, 79); the various narrators in canto XXXIII, however, look back from those days of chivalric heroism on the fall of Roman greatness to forecast an equally millennial future in the Este Ferrara. From the beginning of their wanderings in the rush of an eternal present, the characters may look forward to a chiliastic age that is defined with respect to (and thus will be no better than) a vanished primeval innocence.

> Quindi terran lo scettro i signor giusti,
> che, come il savio Augusto e Numa fenno,
> sotto il benigno e buon governo loro
> ritorneran la prima età de l'oro. . . .
> Alfonso è quel che col saper accoppia
> sí la bontà, ch'al secolo futuro
> la gente crederà che sia dal cielo
> tornata Astrea dove può il caldo e il gielo.

[III, 18, 51]

Then the just lords will hold sway, as wise Augustus and Numa did, for under their benign and good government they will bring back the golden age. . . . Alfonso is the one who joins wisdom and goodness in such a way that in future ages people will believe that Astrea has returned from heaven to where heat and cold are felt.

In the *Satire* Ariosto claimed that he would have done nicely in the days when men lived on acorns, much as Don Quixote

would later do in the face of the dispassionate respect of Sancho
Panza and the dumb amazement of the goat herds who inspire
the soliloquy. His early Latin poem in praise of philosophy is
set in an earthly paradise "cum longo innocuis habitata est
gentibus aevo," (v. 6: "when the earth was inhabited for a long
period by innocent people") and the beginning of the *Cinque
Canti* II praises Saturn, Hercules, and Jove in the golden age of
Greece, India, and Rome; but the passage that immediately follows his Machiavellian observation in this last text (4) is redolent
with sarcasm: after comparing political tyrants of the cinquecento
with Caligula and Nero, he concludes, "Ma se ne tace, perché è
sempre meglio / lasciar i vivi, e dir del tempo veglio" ("but men
are silent about them, because it is always better to leave the
living and speak of older times"). Chrétien de Troyes had taught
that intermittent struggle is the natural lot of the ideal knight,
just as it is a mandate of narrative technique; and at the end of
the *Furioso* a joyous and promising marriage follows a cere-
monious funeral, while the marriage itself is followed by a challenge to the bridegroom to engage in mortal combat. And yet,
beyond technique and chivalric ideology, Ariosto's demur on the
golden age is also as if he realized that even an Arcadian setting
will contain the seeds of its own destruction. So it is that the
seductive city of Alcina is first said to be of gold, then of the
fool's gold of alchemy, then once again to *seem* made of gold, to
the author, who himself seems not yet to have learned his lesson,
because of its glitter.

> e d'oro sia da l'alta cima a terra.
> Alcun dal mio parer qui si dilunga,
> e dice ch'ell'è alchimia: e forse ch'erra;
> et anco forse meglio di me intende:
> a me par oro, poi che sí risplende.
>
> [VI, 59]

And it may be of gold from the summit to the ground. Someone might
differ with my opinion and say it is alchemy: perhaps he is wrong and
again perhaps he understands better than I; to me it seems to be gold
since it shines so.

Ruggiero struggles with the world no man has made, permanently
fresh and strange, yet does not attempt to abandon it. It is not

by chance that he and Orlando are both seduced by "angelici sembianti" (VII, 15).

An acceptable vision of prelapsarian innocence divorced from mundane concerns is further complicated by the impression conveyed by the author that he was somehow privy to the many events he relates and that these events will ineluctably lead to the real present, which is that of his readers or listeners. The reader who wanders unsuspectingly into the world of the *Furioso* is immediately immersed in a world possessed of its own calendar logic and its own shifting planes of temporal reference which are aspects both of the author's concept and technique. Perhaps the most familiar level is the episodic narration of the *cantastorie*. The woman who relates the custom of Pinabello's castle begins, "Come l'usanza (che non è piú antiqua di tre dí) comminciò" (XXII, 49: "Since the custom [which is not older than three days] began"), but the interjection belongs more properly to the author, who partitions his poem into cantos without his characters' knowledge; "not older than three days" translates into "less than three cantos ago," because it was in canto XX that the listeners in Ariosto's imaginary piazza first heard of Pinabello's custom. This time scheme is anything but consistent when Ariosto passes to other conventions and perhaps runs afoul of technical problems. In IX, 7, he takes care to date Orlando's quest for Angelica.

> Tra il fin d'ottobre e il capo di novembre,
> ne la stagion che la frondosa vesta
> vede levarsi e discoprir le membre
> trepida pianta, fin che nuda resta,
> e van gli augelli a strette schiere insembre
> Orlando entrò ne l'amorosa inchiesta

Around the end of October and the beginning of November, in the season when the trembling tree sees its leafy clothing removed and its limbs laid bare, and the birds take off together in tight formation, Orlando set out on his lover's quest.

The resolute search continues into spring. In the next canto (63) we are still in spring, but here it is the eternal spring of the *locus amoenus* that exists outside of time and prevails at Logistilla's castle, where Ruggiero is momentarily safe from Alcina's cunning.

Further on (94) we come across Angelica, who "pur quella matina" ("that very morning")—actually *two* cantos earlier: VIII, 61—had been tied to a rock for the Orca's dinner and who will later be rescued by Ruggiero. Now, there is good reason to believe that the composition of Angelica's rescue by Ruggiero (X, 111) which appeared in the first edition actually postdated Orlando's strikingly similar rescue of Olimpia (XI, 59) which remained in manuscript until the third edition; that the two episodes were originally one but were split in two by substituting names in order to solve technical problems of credibility and inserted material.[13] The major insert seems to have been Ruggiero's trip to Britain in canto X after his liberation from Alcina. Earlier, the good Melissa has assuaged Bradamante's misery: "Le promette e giura, in pochi giorni / far che Ruggiero a riveder lei torni" (VII, 46: "she promises and swears to make Ruggiero return to her in a few days"). The vague temporal limits, preceding both *far* and *riveder* in the poetic syntax, could mean either that Bradamante would see Ruggiero within a few days or, in the event of the transpired diversion to Britain and his momentary passion for Angelica, that Melissa would simply start him on his way within that time period.

The author's control of temporal dimensions in his story seems vague from the beginning, but irresolution does not fail to correspond to the character or situation involved. As the second canto opens, the author chides Love for its injustice: Angelica returns Ruggiero's love with hatred, so much that she "vorria la morte." The vaguely conditional future is in keeping with the hazy existence she both leads and represents, to the point where, after her return to Cathay (XXX, 16), she survives only as a random memory or dream among those who once passionately sought her. Ariosto grants premonitions to her most ardent suitor, Orlando, if only he could see clearly enough to grasp the imagery in which they take shape; in his restless dream before the battle (VIII, 71), the darting shafts of light and their play on water preview his illusive quest of Angelica, and the autumn soulscape of bared limbs quoted above, revealing a cold reality, points unswervingly to Orlando's bestial wanderings and redemption from illusion.[14] Subsequently, Orlando quarrels with Ferraú, who acquires the count's helmet, thus accomplishing a promise he had made earlier to Argalia (I, 30). Ariosto gives us a peek at the future by telling us that Ferraú wore the helmet until Orlando eventually killed him "between two bridges" (XII, 62). But the projected future is in reality a misrepresented past, for Ferraú survives in the *Furioso* (cf. XXXVI, 11), while in the *Morgante* (XXIV, 158), where Ariosto's mind is for the moment, the Saracen's father pardons Orlando for having killed him *sul ponte*. Four stanzas later (66), Ariosto claims to put off "for a long time" his rhymes on Ferraú; although he hastens back to him at the start of canto XIV, the many unrelated events that intervene give us the *impression* that much time has elapsed. So the time-table given to the reader is subject to change without any notice, but at least he sees the immediate future better than the characters. The solicitous author assures us that Ruggiero will eventually recover from the grievous wounds he receives from Mandricardo (XXX, 62); though the assurance cuts the suspense somewhat, we are compensated by an insight that is denied to the characters, who must dwell on surface appearances and cannot read the inevitable chiastic reversal of fortune: "Appare a manifesti segni / vivo che vive, e senza vita il morto . . ." (68: "it appears clearly that the living man is alive and the dead man is without life"). The only characters who are as privileged as the reader—in fact more privileged, except for the elected Ferrarese in Ariosto's audience—are the progenitors of the Estensi line, who from the middle of the poem ever on (XXVI, 39; XXXIII, 6, 65) receive certain tokens of their great progeny.

II   *Of Arms and the Men*

The hero's freedom from the normal constraints of time can be a kind of dreadful freedom that merely accentuates his sense of obligation to overcome preponderant obstacles and to accomplish his mission. If he is to follow his Vergilian prototype and forge the uncreated conscience of his race, he too must "suffer bitterly in battle as he strives to found his city." Ruggiero's enemies must wound him grievously, and Rodomonte, as the devil's surrogate, must loom larger than life. The earth is too small to contain the effects of their actions because these effects also involve God himself (XXX, 49, 54). Ariosto's battle scenes strive for an effect of immediacy:

> Già l'un da l'altro è dipartito lunge,
> quanto sarebbe un mezzo tratto d'arco:
> già l'uno contra l'altro il destrier punge,
> né de le lente redine gli è parco:
> già l'uno e l'altro di gran colpo aggiunge . . .
>
> [XXIII, 82]

Already one has moved away from another, perhaps as much as half the flight of an arrow: already one spurs his horse against another, and neither is sparing in loosening his reins; already both join in trading heavy blows.

They also observe stylized epic conventions that had held firm since the time of Homer. Preparatory to a description of the massed Saracen forces, Ariosto promises at the end of canto XIII to relate "l'ordine e la mostra." This order and review take the form in XIV, 11–28, of the Homeric catalog of ships, but the specific model for actual combat of pagan and Christian alike is the *chanson de geste.* Rodomonte's primitive psychological profile recalls the basic conflict in the *Chanson de Roland* between prowess and wisdom: "E più di cento ne levò di mezzo. / Ma la ragione al fin la rabbia vinse" (XVIII, 23: "and he carried off more than a hundred from their midst. But reason finally conquered rage"); and when Ferraú sees a close friend severed, he is driven to avenge him in a description that preserves the archetypal bloodlust, yet curiously anticipates later chivalric parody:

> gli divide l'elmo da la cima
> per la fronte, per gli occhi e per la faccia
> per mezzo il petto, e morto a terra il caccia.
>
> [XVI, 73]

He splits his helmet from the top through the forehead, through eyes, face, and the middle of his chest, and drives him dead to the ground.[15]

The chivalric ethos of the *Furioso* is fatally different from that in the *chansons de geste*, resembling them in every way except fundamentally. Through most of the poem author and character are oblivious to the *profanum vulgus*—"Non mira Orlando a quella plebe bassa" (IX, 72: "Orlando does not notice this common crowd")—view them as background scenery if they see them at all—"La sciocca turba disïosa attende / ch'i duo buon cavallier vengano in prova" (XXX, 27: "The anxious crowd waits for the two knights to test themselves")—or hold them aggressively in contempt:

> non dirò squadre, non dirò falange,
> ma vulgo e populazzo voglio dire,
> degno, prima che nasca, di morire
>
> [XVI, 23]

I will not say squadrons, I will not say phalanxes, but I mean to say masses and populace, worthy of dying before they are born.[16]

This patrician disdain is severely qualified at the end of the poem when Ruggiero, denied Bradamante's hand by her parents, laments that Fortune did not give him riches to match his merits. The Wheel of Fortune, drawn from a fragment in Horace, becomes assimilated with "il volgo, nel cui arbitrio son gli onori, / che, come pare a lui, li leva e dona" (XLIV, 50: "the herd, in whose judgment honors reside, removes and gives them as it sees fit". In the next *ottava* the author lists the qualities the crowd fails to value—*la beltà, l'ardire, la possanza del corpo, la destrezza, la virtù.* . . . The last term sums up and includes the others—beauty, energy, physical power, cleverness—while, at the same time, it includes but goes well beyond chivalric courage and sense of measure.

As in the medieval romances, characters try to show a combination of courtesy and valor to their loved ones and friends (XIV, 115; XXV, 19), and, as in the *Roland*, opinion differs as to how these attributes should be demonstrated. Unlike Roland,

> . . . Orlando a far l'opre virtuose,
> piú che a narrarle poi, sempre era pronto:
> né mai fu alcun de li suoi fatti espresso,
> se non quando ebbe i testimonii appresso.
>
> [XI, 81]

Orlando was always more ready to do heroic deeds than to relate them afterwards, and never were any of his acts made known except when witnesses were there.

Grifone's categorical imperative is quite the opposite: "Se n'abbia occasïone, /mostrar virtude mai non disconvenne" (XVII, 24: "if

one has the chance, it is never inappropriate to show one's merit");
thus, the wrongful disgrace visited on him by Martano, who was
masquerading in his armor, is all the worse for being a "publica
ignominia" (123; cf. V, 86).[17]

Passive femininity is subject to rules of social decorum and
nature's laws, but adherence to these laws is governed by situation
ethics. When Bradamante approaches the city of Marganorre, she
sees three half-naked ladies and wonders:

> chi sí iniquo fue,
> e sí di legge e di costumi fuora,
> che quei segreti agli occhi altrui riveli,
> che, quanto può, par che Natura celi.
>
> [XXXVII, 29]

Who was so wicked and so beyond law and customs that he would
reveal to the eyes of others these secrets that Nature seems to conceal
as much as possible.

Although we soon hear a speech admonishing death before dishonor (XXXVIII, 4), we learn that these ladies are to be forgiven
for not preferring death because "sempre questo e ogn'altro ob-
brobrio amorza / il poter dir che le sia fatto a forza" (114: "being
able to say that it was done to her by force always mitigates this
and every other infamy"). Nominalizing of *il poter dir* thrusts the
situation from an accidental occurrence into the status of a topic
of courtly debate. *Gestes* of all kinds are graduated according to
whether a knight is superhuman or merely heroic (XLI, 93). In
the midst of these terrible encounters we may easily pardon
Doralice, rather more pragmatic than fickle in shifting her allegiance from a dead Mandricardo to a living Ruggiero, for the
blunt and realistic necessity of seeking asylum in the graces of
a competent knight: "Proveder le convien d'un che gagliardo /
sia notte e dí ne' suoi bisogni, e forte" (XXX, 73: "she had to
provide herself with one who day and night would be strong
and hardy in looking after her needs"). Her candid appraisal of
actions is typical, for in the debate between public and private
show of valor, it is the public that wins out. Grifone, who had
voted this way, is immediately in turn a witness to a public
debate over courtly deeds (XVII, 69). Ermonide might burn over
the vendetta that separates him and Zerbino, but he would not

differ with the premise of his opponent's brief lecture on the subject "a cavalleria non corrisponde / che cerchi dare ad une donna morte" (XXI, 8: "to try to kill a woman is not consonant with chivalry". Likewise, Ruggiero "sa l'usanza antiqua, e [non] di molto erra" (XXX, 50: "knows the old custom and [does not] wander much") by not killing his opponent's horse. Bradamante finds herself flanked by the allegorical personae of Yes, representing the call of duty to assist the French forces, and No, representing the call of her passion for Ruggiero (II, 65); no matter which decision the audience might have her elect, there could be no misunderstanding of the nature of her alternative. Forensic debate over *Sic aut Non* can structure a whole canto, just as it structures individual happenings. The episode in the first canto where Ferraù is sharply rebuked by Argalia for the disparity between the *detto* and the *effetto* of his chivalric promise to deliver Orlando's helmet (28) forms a pendant to Angelica's legalistic absolution of Sacripante in his defeat at the hands of Bradamante (67). Far from being innovative in chivalric narratives, dispute over right and proper conduct is at the heart of *chansons de geste* from the *Roland* on.[18] But as distinct from the debate of Roland and Olivier which sprang from instinctive movements of the soul, Ariosto's characters mince over details and give the impression of protesting too much. And it is the standard-bearer Ruggiero who best exemplifies the cumbersome weight of chivalric honor. His sleep is troubled, not by a debate between religious faith and his allegiance to the French, but by a long, sophistical calculation on how best to preserve "un nome chiaro" and escape a consensus reproach (XXV, 81–88). In the waning moments of the poem, his greatest struggle with his rival Leone is how to outdo him in courteous show (XLVI, 39).[19]

III The War of Love and the Love of War

Military and courtly preoccupations are inextricably bound from the opening verses of the *Furioso*: "Le donne, i cavallier, l'arme, gli amori, / le cortesie, l'audaci imprese io canto" ("The ladies, the knights, the arms, the loves, the courtesies, the brave deeds I sing"). The many pages of critical exegesis that have been devoted to these lines bespeak their suggestive richness and their importance as a keynote to the work they initiate: their dual source in Dante and Vergil both laments a bygone age and promises a heroic future, their presto and largo rhythm anticipates the broader movements of many cantos, and their structure balances love and war—yet in the incipit the former seem to swallow the latter.

Implicit reversal in thematic direction foreshadows reversals of honor and disfame, love and war, that characters will soon experience.[20] Love and war cooperate in defining the prime attributes of the story's heroine, "non men che fiera in arme, in viso bella" (XXXII, 79: "no less proud in arms than beautiful in face"), and conspire against the hero, who has trouble stripping off his armor for his dalliance with Angelica (X, 114). Bradamante may be more exemplary, but Ruggiero is more typical, because the knight stricken by love is fundamentally at odds with his nature and mission. A lovesick Rodomonte, anomalously sailing in a boat instead of riding on horseback, is even more anomalously portrayed by a Petrarchan conceit: "né spegner può, per star ne l'acqua, il fuoco, / né può stato mutar, per mutar loco" (XXVIII, 89: "cannot put out the fire, by being on the water, and cannot change state by changing place").[21] Lovesickness is incongruous because of the carnage that normally surrounds Rodomonte; the boat ride is incongruous because a *cavaliere* is by definition a man astride a charger and whose life on foot is but a fallow interlude until he can be remounted. Just as the soldier on foot is bound to his armament by rhyme and synecdoche that are both comic and literally true, "nudi / che non han tempo di pur tor gli scudi" (XXXI, 80: "naked because they do not have the time to put on their shields"), the contradiction of the *cavaliere senza cavallo* is a basic indignity that afflicts Christian and Saracen alike. Routed by the French, the Moors learn that "chi non ha destrier, quivi s'avede / quanto il mestier de l'arme è tristo a piede" (XXVI, 25: "he who has no horse learns how sad is the profession of arms on foot"). And disparity between Gradasso mounted and Rinaldo unhorsed is at once physical and symbolic: "Non puoi starmi a paro . . . vivi a piè, che non merti cavallo" (XXXI, 97: "you cannot stand on my level . . . live on foot since you do not deserve a horse").[22]

Since rider and horse are so integral to one another, their separation or combination in multiples provides one of the story's basic situation comedies. In I, 22 Ferraú and Rinaldo, rivals in love and war, are brought together by a common need of transportation, a need that underlines the irony of the author's claim that their sharing of one horse was evidence of the "great goodness of the ancient knights." As they amble off, the arithmetical symmetry in the silhouette they present is subverted by the underlying disharmony of their situation: "Da quattro sproni il destrier punto arriva / ove une strada in due si dipartiva" ("goaded by four spurs the horse comes to where one road divided in two"). Although Sacripante hoists Angelica up behind his saddle, "a piú lieto uso" ("for a happier use"), he is soon forced to admit that "un sol ronzin per dui saria mal atto" (71–73: "a single horse is poorly suited for two"). So it is not surprising that Rinaldo should rudely leave Sacripante on foot without even saying "a Dio, non che lo 'nviti in groppa" (II, 19: "God be with you, let alone invite him upon his horse's rump"), or that, immediately before finding the marvelous Hippogriff, the normally unperturbed Astolfo should appear ludicrous chasing the lowly farmer who has stolen his horse: "Gli va dietro correndo a piú potere" (XXII, 12: "he goes running behind him with all his might":).

Beyond horsemanship, identification of man and animal in other respects recalls the countless physiological studies from Leonardo's time on that attempted to establish the organic similarity and unity of living creatures, the ultimate fusion of identities between man and beast. It is natural for Ruggiero to labor under a metaphoric yoke (XLII, 64), and not surprising for Bradamante to insult Rodomonte by calling him *bestial* (XXXV, 42), since he had earlier been likened to a boar, dog, tiger, and wolf. Yet the very syntax describing Orlando's life in the wilds inextricably links man and beast: "Avea di fera, piú che d'uomo, il volto" (XXXIX, 45: "he had the face more of a wild animal than of a man").[23] Verse structure aims at a microcosmic synthesis of the opposing forces that inspire the poem's overall pattern.

Love brings out the animal in man and war turns him into a veritable brute; yet from the knight's vantage point, the most singular threat of modern warfare is not that it equates him with beasts, but rather that it equates him with other men. Gunpowder had, at least, a democratizing effect, though many Renaissance writers found this to be no blessing. Machiavelli discoursed freely on the *arte della guerra*, but Leonardo hesitated to reveal much of his technological weaponry, Agrippa von Nettesheim steadfastly refused to issue his *Pyrographie*, and, at the very time he was declining his titles of nobility, Montaigne saw the use of horses to pull siege engines as a sure token of the iron age ("Des coches"). Ariosto's attitude toward warfare is ambivalent for several reasons. For one, there is the hopeless conflict between the individual chivalric prowess he is praising and modern technology. The fictional mode allows him the luxury of anachronism and of reversing the proportion of fantasy and reality. Most notable among the exponents of firearms is King Cimosco, whom Ruggiero meets and defeats in canto IX. The wide-eyed lady who relates Cimosco's weapon does so with a naïveté appropriate to a medieval observer who would have been transplanted in the sixteenth century (28–29), and when Ruggiero routs his opponent he flies, appropriately, with "more speed than an arrow" (79). He takes possession of the cannon, not for his own use, but to throw it in the sea because only a "soft spirit acts with unfair advantage" (89). In medieval romance the virtuous knight had always triumphed over magic put to bad use, so it is fitting that Alcina, the woman scorned, use artillery (X, 51) and, more significantly, that its invention be ascribed to the devil, be equated with original sin, and be rediscovered for the sixteenth century by a German necromancer (IX, 91; XI, 22–23). Strangely enough, the beginning of the influence of the natural sciences in the Renaissance strengthened the belief in magic. The men to whom the wonders of nature began to be revealed, and the existence of natural forces and laws made evident, were unable at first to distinguish clearly between the possible and the impossible. The very strangeness of the knowledge they were gaining suggested the existence of mysterious unseen powers. Men spoke of natural magic as distinguished from demonic, even of "empirical" magic. And the more they added to their very imperfect knowledge of this world, the more they seemed to cling to the idea of a world beyond. Thus, the story of firearms in the *Furioso* assumes allegorical proportions and symbolizes the evil and idle curiosity that are eternally latent in man. Ariosto's ambivalence toward modern warfare is accentuated by the praise he heaps on Alfonso d'Este for his victory at Ravenna, yet seems to withdraw because of the excessive slaughter visited on the Spanish and papal forces.[24] The narrator strikes a Janus-like pose, then, in his subsequent praise of Ruggiero:

> La forza di Ruggier non era quale
> or si ritrovi in cavallier moderno,
> né in orso né in leon né in animale
> altro piú fiero, o nostrale od esterno.
> Forse il tremuoto le sarebbe uguale,
> forse il Gran diavol; non quel de lo 'nferno,
> ma quel del mio signor, che va col fuoco
> ch'a cielo e a terra e a mar si fa dar loco.
>
> [XXV, 14]

Ruggiero's strength was not what is now found in a modern knight, nor in a bear, nor in a lion nor in another fiercer animal, whether native or foreign. Perhaps the Earthquake would be its equal, perhaps the Great Devil; not the one from Hell, but the one of my lord, which works with fire that makes the sky and the earth and the sea give way.

The "Gran diavolo" and the "Terremoto" were the names given to the cannons of Alfonso d'Este.

The *Furioso* is rife with willful anachronisms that overlay the medieval battlefield with the terminology and actual dimensions of fortifications used in campaigns fought by Alfonso d'Este, and endorse the *contaminatio* with a classical allusion that provides its skeleton.[25] Ariosto's confusion would not have sat badly with his Este patrons, in view of the self-adulation of, for instance, Duke Ercole, who fancied himself an Arthur reincarnate and would-be "cavalliero erante," nor would it have militated against the notion that the poem is a microcosm, a *liber mundi*, embracing all three dimensions of time and space, of which Ferrara is the focal point and earthly paradise to be regained.[26] From the time of Poggio, humanists commonly held that all roads led to the microcosm of Rome and crisscrossed in the history of that eternal city.[27] Ariosto shared yet tempered this view. In the third satire he casts an abstract glance at the world, arbitrarily assigns Morocco, China, Egypt, and Hungary as its parameters with Rome at its center (vv. 199–200); but he is writing from Ferrara where his family and personal affairs, courtly and literary activities, are centered. The 1502 epithalamium to Lucrezia Borgia had balanced Rome and Ferrara in a diptych joined by the theme "all things change." Passing through a world of change, it is the unification of Bradamante and Ruggiero, the resolution of war in love, that makes them the guarantors of the paradise to be found in Ferrara.

CHAPTER 4

Variety, Which is Usually Pleasing to Many

(*Orlando Furioso*, XXII, 3)

NITY in Ariosto's masterpiece cannot be assumed and dismissed in one sentence. The *Furioso* and its vast popularity provided grist for critical debate that extended from the 1550s into the next century.[1] Basically, the polite quarrel pitted advocates of an academic approach to epic poetry against modern proponents of variety within or outside of traditional constraints. Taking Aristotle's *Poetics* at the letter, the "ancients" held that the epic poem should follow the exploits of one single hero through a unified action related in a uniformly elevated style. This had been the case with the *Iliad* and the *Aeneid*, which stood as eternal, requisite, and unsurpassable models for any future poet who wished to undertake an epic narrative. Not one action of many heroes, nor many of one, nor many of many, as Speroni puts it, for these result respectively in history, biography, and dissipation. Some dogmatists like Minturno, running counter to long-standing practice and even to the examples of Homer and Vergil, claimed that unified epic action should be limited to a twenty-four-hour period and should confine its mimetic pattern to one literary model. It is clear that the *Furioso* meets none of these distinctions, except for the one Speroni labeled "vizioso." The apparently indiscriminate mixture of "le donne, i cavallier, l'arme, gli amori, le cortesie, l'audaci imprese" was at the outset a patent breach of unified action. Although the *Odyssey*, in contradistinction to the single thread of the *Iliad*, could be seem as a paradigm for episodic romance, the open end of the *Furioso*, with its marriage that could serve as a prelude to further adventures, lacks the conclusiveness of the return to Ithaca.

The "moderns" who rallied to Ariosto's defense argued that it is nature, including natural gifts of the mind, that is eternal, that modern poets writing in the vernacular can thus rival the classical masters, and that the great popularity of the *Furioso* is at least partial evidence of the author's natural talent. As for broken unity, Giraldi answered Speroni somewhat on his own ground by accounting for the three levels of classical discourse: long narratives, he asserted, can treat the action of one man, many actions of one, or many actions of many men. In line with the belief that romance allowed of multiple plots, Francesco Caburacci lauded Ariosto for having initiated poetry that combined comedy, tragedy, and the epic, thus defending him against the charge of incredibility by pointing to a resultant gain in variety. Variety is manifestly inherent in the natural world which God has created and of whom the poet-creator is the earthly surrogate. But before theology, pleasing variety was justified in literary terms by citing the Horatian adage that the poet who mixes the useful and the sweet wins applause and by pointing to the Ciceronian injunction to teach, move, and please. A letter to Lorenzo Loredan suggests that Ariosto preferred to adhere especially to the third quality in composing a work that deals with "cose piacevoli e delectabeli de arme e de amore" ("pleasing and delightful things of arms and love"), although such pleasing in no way excludes teaching.[2] Since poetry had to come to terms with the onus laid on it by Plato of being a delightful lie, moralistic critics felt obliged to legitimize its sweet and pleasing attributes by stressing its useful teachings, and, next to outright didacticism, the most direct way to teach was through allegory. Thus, from the 1540s glosses and marginal commentaries accompanied editions of the *Furioso* or themselves constituted separate, explanatory volumes. The most notable of these were Simon Fornari's *Sposizione sopra l'Orlando Furioso* (1549) and Oratio Toscanella's *Belleze del Furioso* (1574). After all, Ariosto's sources had received similar attention; the *Vita Caroli Magni et Rolandi* of the so-called pseudo Turpin was allegorized, and even the *Morgante* came to bear allegorical readings. Orazio Ariosto held that teaching and pleasing came together at the allegorical level in his great-uncle's masterwork, and later takeoffs on Ariosto tended to make Ruggiero into a representation of certain abstract qualities, something like Alcina or Angelica, in view of the uncertain personality he seems to have in the *Furioso*. So where Ariosto had portrayed a multifaced world bathed in chiaroscuro, now supraliteral, single "meanings" were sometimes ascribed to events and characters.

One further argument that Ariosto's defenders might have advanced in support of the self-consistency of his work, but did not, is that the heterogeneous form he elected conforms to the arabesque vision of reality that motivates it. The apparent stasis of love and war at the poem's solemn conclusion belies the ambivalent countercurrents in the poet's attitude throughout the length of his work toward the war of the sexes. This war had been extensively fought in the Middle Ages and had so penetrated the language of love as to constitute its main stock of clichés: the lover pursues, besieges, and finally overcomes his lady, who, in courtly versions, makes him a prisoner to her charms (cf. XXIV, 30). In the Renaissance of Northern Italy the position of woman in the world went beyond an object of valorous assault. Her capacity for disinterested love was itself the subject of lively court debate, with subtle and witty cases put forward on both sides, because in cultural showcases like Urbino and Ferrara women had attained an intellectual and social parity with men: "Se le carte sin qui state e gl'inchiostri / per voi non sono, or sono a' tempi nostri" (XXXVII, 7: "If before this paper and ink have not been for you, now in our time they are"). Classical prototypes like Homer's Penthesilea and Vergil's Camilla were viewed as parallels to the heroism of Caterina Sforza, to the tenacity of Isabella d'Este, and above all to the devotion of Vittoria Colonna (cf. XXXI, 61, for "ancient times"). Heroines like Salomé, Judith, and Delilah were favored subjects of painting and emblemata. Many writers created dialogue situations in which characters expounded opposing views on the relative worthiness of women, but Ariosto is perhaps the only one to espouse both sides with apparently equal conviction.[3] An individual figure like Angelica hardly counts in assessing the author's attitude toward womankind—if for the moment we may equate author and narrator—because her voyeurism and heartlessness stand primarily as ironic commentaries on this "angelic semblance" (I, 49; XII, 27) that serves as a register for the ethereal values men invest in her. It is, rather, in following his sweeping generalizations that we become the most aware of his conspicuous inability to tread a straight line in transcribing his true beliefs. In the overture to canto XXII, the narrator claims that the demands of his story for pleasing variety momentarily necessitate a story in dispraise of women, but in return for this one he promises to praise a hundred (3). "One-in-a-hundred" is not the true proportion of good and bad women in the world, as Satyrane alleges in *Faerie Queene* III, vii, but is here simply a manner of speaking to regain the favor of the ladies in the author's audience. The narrator continues to hedge a declaration of his position when Doralice sizes up Mandricardo as a superior warrior and spurns Rodomonte. As he wanders off through the wilds, Rodomonte's lament against women, "miser chi ti crede" (XXVII, 117: "miserable is he who believes you"), is related to us by the disembodied narrator as the echo of a fictional character. At the end of the tirade the narrator explains that his character was wrong, because for every bad one "one must believe" ("creder si dee") there are a hundred good ones. In successive retreats and advances in his position, he tells us that he just happens to have found only the bad but attributes this to his bad luck. He is able to maintain his faith in women against all experience only by a leap of faith. So it is that in introducing the story of Astolfo, Giocondo, and Fiammetta at the beginning of the next canto he protests loud and long over including it, although he admits it is not essential to his work, and thus piques our curiosity. He finally dismisses its validity because it is only fiction and folly—like most other love stories in the *Furioso*.

Ariosto's position is further blurred by the inevitable result of sexual equality: the tendency to transpose attributes of both sexes. The very indecision over the nature of common qualities (*Il Cortegiano*, III, 4) shows that transposition was broadly based in some quarters. Shift in scene from Mitylene in the first version of *La Cassaria* to Sybaris in the second implicitly makes the thinly veiled Ferrara a center of sybaritism and supports Folcio's attack on the effeminate customs of men (V, iii). Later in *La Scolastica* Bonifacio chides Claudio for his unmanly soul and receives the laconic answer "no so s'io l'habbia maschio o femina" (II, v: "I do not know if mine is masculine or feminine"). At the opposite pole, the Renaissance revered the virago, like Tasso's Clorinda, Spenser's Britomart, and Ariosto's Marfisa and Bradamante. The suspenseful introduction of Marfisa in XXVI, 8, and Ariosto's play with pronouns underline the dual role she plays: "Costei (non piú costui detto vi sia)" ("She [who will no longer be called he]"). When she goes to the land of the Alessandrian women and must give evidence of battle worthiness or of sexual potency, Ariosto's banter with the reader needs no Freud to expound it: "dove non l'aitasse la natura, / con la spada supplir stava sicura" (XIX, 69: "where nature did not help her, she was sure to compensate with her sword"). The uninflected praise of women at the outset of canto XX, with Marfisa as its reference point, later becomes clouded by the willful exchange of appearance for reality in the episodes that involve her. In stanza 124 she challenges the less heroic Zerbino in order to force his admission that the old hag Gabrina, looking "like a monkey" in her beautiful dress, is in fact beautiful, and to make him her champion should Marfisa lose; chiastic structure here in Ariosto's line is adequate to the situation, "per riportarne una vittoria poi, / che giovi al vinto, e al vincitore annoi" ("to carry off a victory afterwards that pleases the conquered and annoys the victor"). The equivalent joust over Ate in Spenser (IV, 4) entirely lacks these complications. With theme and variations, Bradamante's exploits are akin to Marfisa's, beginning with the first knight she unhorses dressed like a man (I, 69; XX, 129), and the same antagonism between "femina gentile" and "uomo vile" (XXV, 30). The startling resemblance between her and Ricciardetto that Ariosto presses (XXXVI, 13) allows them to play the game of *Suppositi* with the unsuspecting Fiordispina, who, enamoured of Bradamante, smuggles her into her room dressed as the woman she really is. Later, Ricciardetto accomplishes his quid pro quo by dressing as a woman, passing himself off as Bradamante, and satisfies Fiordispina, none the wiser, by concocting a story about sexual transformation (XXV, 40–64).

Crossover between social and conceptual groups that had previously been distinct, forces circumspection in speaking of allegory and meaning behind surface events. The prime critical fallacies of commentators on Ariostan allegory were the assumptions, as with Lodovico Dolce, that the allegorical strand remains unbroken throughout the *Furioso*, that univalent and unbending meanings can be attributed to any event or object, and that allegorical episodes can be detached from the work and explained apart from the main flow of its action. In the first place, Ariosto seldom conjures up characters whose names and epithets limit their attributes, and when he does they generally serve as static background. When Alcina fires her canon on Ruggiero, Logistilla sends him Andronica (Fortitude), Fronesia (Prudence), Dicilla (Justice), and Sofrosina (Temperance), the four cardinal virtues that were identified with the four streams that watered the garden of paradise. As opposed to, let us say, Spenser's Artegall and Guyon, who respectively exemplify the latter virtues, Ariosto practically drops these four characters from sight while blending and distributing their qualities at various times among various characters. In canto XIV God conspires with Discord to create an "aspro concerto, orribile armonia" (134) among the Saracens; the *merveilleux chrétien*, the allegorical, and the epic thus interact in the same universe but coexist on separate levels which the poet treats unequally at his pleasure in his own creation. In the second place, the meaning and value an object is made to bear may fluctuate according to the person who wields it or the use to which it is put. In this way Renaissance philosophers distinguished among the varieties of magic, both black and white; Alfonso's marvelous canon, for instance, is at once more credible and less diabolic than Alcina's. Perhaps nothing better points up the danger and difficulty of single-minded glossing than Atlante's shield with its fusion of strength and glitter. Such glossing is treacherous since there are in reality two additional shields in the story: Hector's enchanted shield and the *ricco scudo d'oro* with its sibylline prophecy of the Italian wars. Clemente Valvassori gives a circumscribed definition of the brilliant shield,[4] but Fornari insists that the significance of the shield depends on its use and, in a way, on the attitude of the character using it. Such latitude of meaning is appropriate to: 1, II (Atlante's benevolent wish to spare Ruggiero the danger of battle, which, however, diminishes his valor); 2, II–III (Bradamante's wish to employ the magic ring against the power of the magic shield in order to free Ruggiero); 3, VI (his refusal to use the shield in order to exercise his *virtù* against Alcina's forces); 4, VIII, X (his eventual harmless use of it against Alcina's guards so as not to harm dumb animals with his more potent sword, Balisarda, and against her black magic); 5, X (his proper use of it against the unnatural Orc); and 6, XXII (his accidental use of it against the noble Grifone, Aquilante, and Guidon, which leads him to throw it away like Cimosco's canon).

I *Into the Light Above and Down to the World of Gloom*

The invocation of Discord has the effect of opening a Pandora's box of proliferating evils that leaves few corners of the *Furioso* untouched. Immediately after the epithetic description of "Discordia altiera" ("proud Discord") in XVIII, 26, appropriately set in a monastery where the archangel Michael found her, we witness her division into Pride and Discord proper. Love succeeds in fighting off Pride and Discord (XXIV, 114) in an emblematic scene reminiscent of the wall paintings in the Palazzo Schifanoia where gods cavort in courtly dress. But with the advent of the shield of gold, pride and discord lose their allegorical magnitude and return insidiously in lowercase to plague the French forces and incite them to compete for individual glory.

The connection between pride and fame was well known to Renaissance poets. Petrarch assured man that fame saved him from the tomb and gave him life (*Triumphus fame*, v. 9). Speaking of the Italian scene and its wars, Sannazaro countered by inviting man to leave his fame in the "tenebrosa tomba," and, imitating a sonnet that Petrarch had imitated from Catullus, he ironically enjoined: "Scriva chi fame al mondo aver non vòle" ("Let him write who does not wish worldly fame"). While to some *Roma aeterna* stood as an exemplum, inviting man to recreate its glory, to others the ambition that led the empire beyond the breaking point gave evidence that pride goes before a fall.[5] Like other poets who went to school to the classics, Ariosto knew that *fama* in Vergil bore the twin meaning of glory and ill repute. In "Ad Herculem Strozzam" fame tells how poets draw their eloquence from the Hippocrene, but the poet goes on to say that false fame usually relates good things whereas true fame relates the bad (vv. 9–14). Beyond the dichotomy of normative rhetoric between *laus et vituperatio*, praise and blame, poets, kings, and heroes all faced the more serious alternatives of fame or oblivion.

Ariosto's characters move constantly between these extremes. Medoro, who eventually goes off with Angelica to their Indian kingdom, is one of the few characters that manages to combine pride and humility. In XVIII, 169, the faithful vassal sets out behind enemy lines to find and bury his lord Dardinello in order to ensure his lord's fame. Solicitous of his own name should Fortune deny his success, he instructs his companion Cloridano to remain behind as a witness: "Per fama almeno il mio buon cor si scuopra" ("My good courage will be at least revealed by fama"). Cloridano interposes that he too prefers death to dishonor—"anch'io famosa morte amo" (171: "I too love a famous death"). Seeking their own renown, they steal into the French camp and become Fortune's agents in denying fame to others who die anonymously.

> Quattro altri uccide appresso all'indovino,
> che non han tempo a dire una parola:
> menzion dei nomi lor non fa Turpino,
> e 'l lungo andar le lor notizie invola:

Near to the magician he killed four others who do not have time to speak a word: Turpin does not mention their names, and the long road steals their renown.

Irony in this situation—a tragic or comic irony, according to whether or not we take the question of fame seriously—arises from the inability of characters to see themselves or one another as we see them. With a wistful sigh over the envious fate of his brothers, Guidon ends his lament on the life of slothful sensuality he is forced to lead: "La fama del mio sangue spiega i vanni / per tutto 'l mondo, e fin al ciel s'estolle" (XX, 63: "The fame of my blood spreads its wings through all the world, and reaches the sky"). He might have chosen a different metaphor if he had known the allegory of Time which Astolfo learns on the moon. Rich names that enjoyed great fame on earth are there carried along by the river of forgetfulness into which two swans dip their beaks; "alcun' ne salvan gli augelli benigni: / tutto l'avanzo oblivïon consume" (XXXV, 15: "the benevolent birds save some: oblivion consumes all the rest"). Correspondingly, the narrator's own voice must be shaded by the irony of the preceding allegory, or is at least ambiguous, when he later addresses women and refers to Ercole II:

> . . . che spiega l'ali come
> canoro cigno, e va cantando a volo,
> e fin al cielo udir fa il vostro nome.
>
> [XXXVII, 13]

Who spreads out his wings like a melodious swan, and goes singing as he flies, and makes your names heard up to the sky.

The allegory of Time, then, informs our understanding of events that precede and follow it, because every earthly occurrence finds its mirrored image in heaven: identical yet reversed. It becomes, as it were, a concave mirror, "di folle audacia specchi" ("mirrors of foolish audacity"), a microcosm that intensifies by concentrating its reflection of earthly concerns. So when Marganorre is compared to Nero in XXXVII, 43, thus balancing the praise of women in that canto with blame of men, we are brought back thematically to canto XXXV. Saint John had explained that the flock of crows, vultures, magpies, and other raucous birds represent fawning courtiers, liars, and detractors, but the swans that succeed in preserving one name in a hundred thousand for the temple of immortality represent poets. The Evangelist's sudden admonition to the great princes of the world who blame virtue and praise vice is ironic for being out of context and out of character. He argues that the reputation of Augustus would not be so good nor Nero's so bad if they had had different attitudes toward encouraging and supporting poets; that Aeneas, Achilles, and Hector were not as noble as Vergil and Homer made them appear; and that in fact Homer falsified the facts and outcome of the Trojan war (22–27; cf. XVIII, 1). Saint John's tirade is not so inappropriate, however, if we read it as a speech set within a larger speech, where Ariosto obliquely addresses a warning to Ippolito and promises to falsify history and lie on his behalf. After all, he had already lied for the ladies in his audience, and implicitly lied for Ippolito in XXXV, 8, as Homer and Vergil did for Hector, the conventional ancestor of Ruggiero and thus of the cardinal.

Ippolito would not have needed Saint John's patient exegesis, because the allegory is a skillful amalgam of commonplaces that were known to any educated audience. Opposition of swan to crow and magpie and the loss of fortune in the river Lethe occur in close proximity in the *Satire* (III, 142–44, 169–71; IV, 106), and Temples of Immortality, Houses of Fame, are too numerous to mention.[6] As allegorical readings illuminated exemplary virtue in the classics and aligned them with Christian teachings, as New Comedy censured common vices, and as tragedy dramatized the ultimate triumph of virtue over vice in the lives of kings and heroes, the Renaissance commonplace was meant to have a universal application yet came to be an encomium in praise of highly placed individuals, their lineage and valiant deeds. The universality of the commonplace derived in part from the notion, taken up by Petrarch (*De vita solitaria*, II, ix, 6) and later humanists that literature was copious enough to contain the whole world and that the writer was like a hunter stalking by a kind of local motion through the labyrinth of the human microcosm—the three cavities of the mind from the anterior seat of common sense and/or imagination to the central lobe of judgment to the posterior ventricle of memory—in search of his idea.[7] This physiological scheme of intellectual and affective life assumes large proportions in the macrocosm of the *Furioso*. The heart is the battleground where simplistic emotions are harmonized by attaining equilibrium or by driving out their opposite; but metaphors of the mind like the prison of love or Atlante's castle are the loci where men lose rather than find themselves or one another, for "il desiderio uman non è tutto uno" (XIII, 50: "human desire is not all one"). The knight errant and his lady wandering in the world of the mind are entrapped by a logic of cause and effect that does them in: "De le quai non più tosto entrò le porte, / che fu sommersa nel commune errore" (79: "As soon as she entered its doors she was plunged into the common error").

The path the characters tread in the journey of their life is a timeworn cliché to which Ariosto gives masterful variations that bear on the theme and structure of his work. *La strada* functions equally as a metaphor of prideful aspiration to fame and of the failure that engulfs human endeavor. A minor character fears

> che 'l fratello a pericolo non vada,
> o come è pur commun disio, cercando
> di spïar sempre ciò che ad altri accada
>
> [V, 48]

That his brother is going into danger [down the dark road], as in fact there is a common wish to do, always trying to discover what pertains to others.[8]

But Rodomonte is so

> indomito, superbo e furibondo,
> che d'ire al ciel no tarderebbe a notte,
> quando la strada si trovasse al mondo
>
> [XIV, 119]

indomitable, proud and ferocious, who would not delay until night to go to the sky if the road were found in the world.

When Ruggiero's guide takes the symbolically shorter road in search of Rodomonte, who has taken the longer road, the characters pass like ships in the night, thus underlining the common error and enabling the author to save their confrontation for the climax of his work. The conventional choice, however, between the harsh road of virtue and the easy road of vice, exemplified emblematically by Hercules at the crossroads of life,[9] does not hold for the characters who are deceived from the outset as to the nature of the road they choose. The aimless (one might even say metaphysical) wandering of the knights is so central to the meaning of the *Orlando Furioso* that Ariosto initiates and pursues it at the earliest opportunity. Orlando loses Angelica, only a moment after regaining her, to which the narrator intones, "Ecco il giudicio uman come spesso erra!" (I, 7: "this is how often human judgment errs [wanders]").[10] The wispy Angelica is also sought by Ferraú, who, not knowing which way to turn, circles back in futility to his point of departure (23). Meanwhile, she flees through dark and frightening forests, "di qua di là" (33: "this way and that").

Purposeless ambling "this way and that" is the most frequent kind of movement and action that take place in the story's recurring "dark forest"; by the way they associate isolated characters and centralize disparate meanings, the rhythm of fluctuation and the place of darkness cannot be considered separately, although they may occur individually. Whether taken separately or together, both action and its locale have received extensive critical commentary in an attempt to trace their ancestry back through Boccaccio, Petrarch and Dante, Augustine, Horace, and Vergil.[11] Chaucer, Statius, Lucan, and Ovid might have been added to the unending list. These correlatives vary in Ariosto with altered narrative demands, but retain the same sense of fate which misleads man in a foreign world that baffles him: "Per errore / di via o di mente, qui tua sorte guida" (XXXI, 66: "by error of road or mind, your fate leads here"), as Rodomonte puts it. Paradoxically, the "di qua di là" of the sea that grips Rinaldo's boat as it leaves Calais (II, 30) and Astolfo's boat as it approaches (XXII, 10) confers a permanence on the natural world at the same time that it denies it to man. Orlando tossing in his sleep, troubled by the prismatic sparkle of light on water which is the essence of Angelica, "or quinci or quindi" (VIII, 71: "now this way, now that"), is a foreshadowing of his madness. The narrator reduces this wandering to primitive equations, "or per li campi or per le selve tenne: / e sí come era uscito di se stesso, / uscí di strada" (XII, 86: "now through the fields, now through the forests he went: and as though he had gone out of his mind, he left the road"), and finally explains it discursively (although we have long since guessed) at the precise center of his poem:

> Gli è come una gran selva, ove la via
> conviene a forza, a chi vi va, fallire:
> chi su, chi giú, chi qua, chi là travia.
>
> [XXIV, 2]

It is like a great forest to him, where the road must necessarily mislead whoever goes there: one up, one down, one here, one there goes astray.

The forest is always near at hand to the characters and is always open to them, except when they seek it expressly (XLIII, 131). They do not know how they get there, like the emotions that overtake them, and they do not seem to know how they get out:

> E tanto gli occupò la fantasia
> il nativo odio, il dubbio e la paura,
> ch'inavedutamente uscí di via:
> e ritrovossi in una selva oscura
>
> [II, 68]

His inbred hatred, doubt, and fear so occupied his imagination that, unawares, he left the road and found himself in a dark wood.

> Di qua di là si volse, né persona
> incontrò mai da domandar la via.
> Si trovò uscir del bosco in su la nona
>
> [XXIII, 20]

She turned this way and that, and never met anyone of whom to ask the way. She found that she was leaving the wood around noon.

Variety Which is Usually Pleasing to Many

The forest is a utopia like the *locus amoenus* in that it is unlike and exists apart from the normal topography and real geography the characters traverse elsewhere, and, although it stresses the relativity of man's quest, it too is characterized by its absolute components:

> Nel più tristo sentier, nel peggior calle
> scorrendo va, nel più intricato bosco,
> ove ha più asprezza il balzo, ove la valle
> è più spinosa, ov'è l'aer più fosco
>
> [XLII, 52]

He hurries along the most miserable path, the worst road, in the densest wood, where the precipice is harshest, where the valley is thorniest, where the air is gloomiest.

But it recurs more frequently than the paradisiac setting as a reminder of man's universal tendency to err. Like the glittering façade of Alcina's castle, the forest has the eternal seduction of offering all things to all men, without any sense of eventual gratification. The "bosco aventuroso" (XLII, 46), where the knight hopes "now here, now there" to find "strane aventure" (IV, 54)—as indeed he must since his valor must be continually reaffirmed if it is to exist at all [12]—assumes an ironic cast when we recall that *Aventura* is the fickle helpmate of Fortune, who humbles the proud. The forest, then, is also for the knight a place of melancholy and death (XLV, 91–92).

The forest where Orlando discovers that Angelica has been unfaithful to the heavenly ideal he invested in her is metaphorically the same hellish forest where he wanders insane. Laws of chivalry traditionally protected mad knights, but not from the supreme folly which is the entrapment of unbounded love: "The highest happiness becomes the cause of misery, and the perfection of knowing is the cause of folly," as Leonardo put it in another context.[13] This is not the love of Bradamante that transcends individual personality and is ratified by history, nor even the love "that moves the sun in heaven and all the stars," for divine love is sanctioned and accepted by a compromise of faith and reason, imagination and will, no matter how much their proportions may vary or its astronomy may change in the waning medieval mind. The medieval and Renaissance physiology of the brain mentioned earlier divides yet links the faculties of the mind. In that scheme, imagination, the picture-making faculty and "mistress of error and falsity," must be tempered by common sense and by reason in order to keep man from being a victim of appearances. In the *Furioso* the principal victim is Orlando, who, possessed—in both senses of the word—of the shimmering image of Angelica, wandered too far from the middle road. Orlando's *fantasia* is associated with notions of the grotesque, the eccentric and the whimsical, all of which express different nuances of its central meaning, that of an extravagant and impossible deviation from nature. As a hero of romance he transcends natural law because in struggling he displays his surpassing virtues; but when he does the same thing as a figure of fantasy, he displays only his physical power to overcome nature. The man who holds Angelica's ring holds reason and can see reality beyond pretense and art (VIII, 2).

The narrator himself appeals to the "clear light of reason" in addressing an audience that has overcome folly (VII, 2; cf. XVI, 4, and XVII, 117); if he appears to wander to and fro in exposing his attitude toward women in the same audience, it is simply because he too is unlucky in love and to that extent shares Orlando's folly and incarceration (XXX, 1–3). The "madness" and "prison" of love have long since acquired the flat and immediately figurative meanings of clichés, but in Ariosto's day may have had literal and covert referents. Moreover, in our age of sophisticated realism madness is integrated into an everyday structure of thought, and its cosmic mystery has been removed insofar as the dark side of the mind has been progressively revealed. No longer do we instinctively accept a metaphysical frame of reference by which the fool is related to a cosmic and basic phenomenon—a relationship that was only beginning to vanish in Ariosto's time.[14] Published seven years before the first edition of the *Furioso*, the *Praise of Folly* begins to lose the transcendent reference of the fool and to represent a dialectical path to divine Reason, the ultimate denouement in the human comedy. It is only when Bradamante rationalizes an action within the accepted courtly ethic that love is equated with sense, and then only in terms of intelligence (XXXVIII, 3). For the most part, the shadow of madness follows all those who love without measure. Angelica or the author (we are never sure which) views her pursuers

Orlando and Ferraú as "insensati e sciocchi" (XII, 34: "senseless and stupified") as they exchange insults—"Uom bestiale," "pazzo," "matto" (40–41: "Bestial man," "madman," "fool")—not realizing that all terms apply equally to both of them. The figurative "ceppi e la catena" ("fetters and chain") of a generalized humanity "chi in amor s'invecchia" ("whoever grows old in love") in the proem on Orlando's madness is soon taken literally in the punishment of Odorico for his uncontrolled passion (XXIV, 2, 27, 30).

Man's inability to steer a resolute course of action, and the madness of love that deprives him of freedom, are the profane analogues, and in their own right are no less serious, to the theological debate on free will that was to rage throughout the century. Although Ariosto's satire to Bembo dismissed Luther for his tendency to dwell on subtle points, the thrust and language of the apostrophe to unjust Love resembles the Pauline war of contrary forces within man which engaged the critical eyes of Luther, Erasmus, and Calvin as well.

> Ingiustissimo Amor, perché si raro
> corrispondenti fai nostri desiri?
> onde, perfido, avvien che t'è sí caro
> il discorde voler ch'in duo cor miri? [15]

[II, 1]

Most unjust Love, why do you make our desires correspond so rarely [love and hate]? How does it happen that the discordant desires you see in two hearts pleases you so?

Unlike Rabelais' Abbaye de Thélème, for which men and women abandon the constraints of the outside world in order to do as they wish, the characters who are held in Atlante's castle are freed only by Brunello's magic ring, and even then "furon di lor molte a chi ne dolse: che tal franchezza un gran piacer lor tolse" (IV, 39: "there were many of them who were saddened by it; for such freedom deprived them of great pleasure"). Divine intervention to bestow freedom is only tentative—"Dio vi provederà d'aiuto forse, / per liberarvi d'ogni atto villano" ("Perhaps God will provide you with help, to free you from all villainous acts")—and the exercise of choice is guided by reasons that are more pragmatic than moral, ethical, or theological: "E se pure avverrà che poi si deggia / morire, allora il minor mal s'elleggia" (XXIV, 84: "and if finally it happens that you must die, then the lesser evil should be chosen").[16] Saint John's explanation that madness is the most plentiful item on earth (XXXIV, 81) confirms the author's thesis that "natura inchina al male" (XXXVI, 1: "nature inclines to evil"). Thus, Ariodante's congenital and universally shared attraction to danger grants him free will only in making the ultimate decision "di volontaria sua libera morte" (V, 48, 57: "of death by his own free will"). Men are constrained to choose the path they least desire or, conversely, are free to elect only the course that does them in.

II If These are Dreams . . .

Even if the author exclaims, "Oh sommo Dio, come i giudicii umani / spesso offuscati son da un nembo oscuro!" (X, 15: "O mighty God, how human judgment is often hidden by a dark cloud"), and the characters themselves allow that only God has the clear light of prescience (XIX, 103), they at least have the illusion of finding their own way. But this bare allowance is qualified by Ariosto's complex ironies. Heaven responds indifferently to individual characters—"mostrando lor la taciturna diva / la dritta via col luminoso corno" (XLIII, 166: "the silent goddess with the luminous horn showed them [Brandimarte and Orlando] the right way") and to their rivals: "Se no traea fuor d'una nube oscura, / a' prieghi di Medor, la Luna il corno" (XVIII, 183: "if the Moon had not brought out her horn from a dark cloud at Medoro's prayers"), his conquest of fame would have come to nothing and he would never have won Angelica. Not only does the changing visage of the moon justify whatever realism may be in these episodes where characters move from doubt to assurance through her graces, but her ability to coexist in the heavens with her opposite number, Venus, and her capacity as the Three-Faced-Goddess to symbolize indiscriminately heaven, earth, and hell, make her the preeminent emblem of earthly mutability in a poem where lovers make and break alliances with abandon. Living on the crescent of the moon was taken during the Renaissance as a proverbial synonym for living on the crest of Fortune's wheel (cf. Rabelais, I, 9). Thus, the displacement of the transcendent sun by the horns of the moon, a replacing of doubt with hope in one context, elsewhere shifts to the opposite emotional phase: "Quando il mio sol di sé mi priva, / mi leva incontra il rio timor le corna" (XLV, 37: "When my sun deprives me of himself, wicked fear raises his horns against me"; cf. I, 52). The image of light may be used as a facile synonym, of Homeric vintage, for the life-force, and may also play a metonymic role in projecting the viewpoint of the lover who sees his beloved's eyes or Angelica as the play of light among shadows. But unreflected light, conceived as perfect unity and understanding, is the eternally denied goal toward which men grope in the dark night of their soul. As fallen and naturally fallible beings, it is not surprising to see them as individual creatures of the night who blindly strike friend and foe with undifferentiated blows in apocalyptic scenes where the sun is obscured and stars appear at midday, where kings use the cover of night to escape, and where the poet himself cannot see the extent of his own creation.[17]

Personae in the *Furioso*, and its readers, move about in a total spectrum, not of light and darkness, but rather of greater or lesser shadows, constantly struggling for perspective. The Dantesque allusions that embrace the work do not conveniently situate it in a hierarchic progression from hell to heaven, though references to those dimensions are persistently pressed on the reader's awareness. Astolfo's observation from the moon conforms to the contemporary state of optical science,[18] but is even more significant for the way it continues the theme of "il mondo sottosopra volto" and for the lunar perspective it will soon afford on earthly transience.

> Quivi ebbe Astolfo doppia maraviglia:
> che quel paese appresso era sí grande,
> il quale a un picciol tondo rassimiglia
> a noi che lo miriam da queste bande;
> e ch'aguzzar conviengli ambe le ciglia,
> s'indi la terra e 'l mar ch'intorno spande
> discerner vuol; che non avendo luce,
> l'imagin lor poco alta si conduce.
>
> [XXXIV, 71]

There Astolfo had a double surprise: that close up that land was so large, which seems like a little circle to us who observe it from these bounds, and that he has to furrow his brows if he wishes to discern from there the earth and the sea that surrounds it; because, not having any light, their image is not carried far above.

By the same token, we can dismiss in jocularity the significance of Rinaldo's desire to send enemies "giú ne l'inferno / a dar notizia del viver moderno" (XVI, 83: "down to hell to give news of modern life"; cf. XXXIV, 10) only if we discount the frequency of the topos, going back to Aeneas' descent to hades, of travelling to the netherworld to report or receive information on earthly happenings.

Like the flux of temporal dimensions we observed in the last chapter, spatial dimensions in the *Furioso* revolve around a constantly moving center, and in the same way the alterations shape the reader's sense of narrative perspective. Like the Renaissance painter who seems to place himself outside of his picture which, however, reflects him in the act of painting, Ariosto is not much help to his reader in establishing a focal point. His dialogues treat matters of ultimate human concern, but like a Chinese box involve people who quote other people at two or three removes from an illusive (or illusory) original source. In his exordia Ariosto creates a raconteur in his own image, and invests him with an outlook that is commensurate with the fictional cosmos he relates, in which he is already implicated and of which he shares many of the experiences and emotions. The paradoxical views he espouses create a flexibility that is adequate to a world in which magicians, mortal heroes, satanic beings, and personified emotions all mingle, and furnish readers with the clue that understanding and appreciation depend on a simultaneous grasp of the whole, not just of successive and antithetical attitudes. When Rinaldo squares off against an unknown knight in canto XXXI and muses at length on his opponent's courage and prowess, Ariosto takes pains to contrast repeatedly the known and the unknown, the "cavallier estrano" and "il signor di Montalbano." Suspense is prolonged (8–29) as night slowly falls on their increasingly confused combat until the decisive moment when the narrator reveals—to us, not to Rinaldo—that "questo guerriero era Guidon Selvaggio" ("this warrior was Guidon Selvaggio"). Although we may for the moment be surprised, we have already covered this ground. In canto XIX Marfisa fought well into the night against an admirable champion who for thirty-eight octaves is described only as "quel dal nero" ("the one in black"). Finally, in XX, 5, he tells the others he is of the House of Clermont, relates his ancestors, travels, and exploits before dramatically declaring, "Nominato son io Guidon Selvaggio, / di poca pruova ancora e poco noto" ("I am called Guidon Selvaggio, still of little accomplishment and little fame"). The reader draws a mental line between these points and forms a composite profile of the achievements and fame of Guidon, who for the characters remains for a long time a freshly provoked mystery. We have a consistent profile of the less admirable doings of Ruggiero, whose desire to roam the earth is excused by the poet on the basis of the idle curiosity of universalized man (X, 72) and whose infidelity to Bradamante (XXX, 86) is implicitly pardoned by the case histories in the two previous cantos of the reciprocal infidelities of men and women; but at the same time the author may be apologizing for his own work and for the digressions which delayed Ruggiero's return and which Ariosto no doubt did not anticipate in the original conception of his poem.

In those isolated moments when characters are sufficiently astute to pool all sources of information and to synthesize all perception, mistrusting any one sense, they gain insight into the mutability of truth on earth, with its fine calibrations of beauty and ugliness, laughter and tears (XVII, 68, XLIII, 132, 135). But the wisdom this insight may bring consists in renouncing ultimate knowledge, in the realization that in the human condition ignorance may be bliss. Thus, when the Mantuan knight offers Rinaldo the "nappo incantato" that will dispel any lingering doubts about his wife's faithfulness or infidelity, he hesitates and then declines. Before his refusal, the author comments on the complex insight that will soon be Rinaldo's.

> Il signor de la casa allora alquanto
> sorridendo, a Rinaldo levò il viso;
> ma chi ben lo notava, più di pianto
> parea ch'avesse voglia che di riso.
>
> [XLII, 99]

Smiling slightly, the lord of the house raised his face to Rinaldo; but to anyone who was watching him well it seemed that he wanted to cry more than to laugh [cf. XXXV, 47].

This is the sight conferred by wisdom and hard won by long experience. Others, however, hold too literally to the notion that seeing is believing. The aspiring Petrarchan lover who places his faith in the eyes, "windows of the soul," does so by forgetting that centuries of Church fathers and humanist philosophers alike declared that sight is the most reliable of the five senses, which are nevertheless all fallible, and that in seeking ultimate truth in this world man sees "as through a glass darkly (cf. I, 56; VII, 28, 68–69). Rinaldo had an early lesson in cantos V and VI in the waywardness of sight when he saved Ginevra from being unjustly condemned—a case of *I Suppositi* transformed into tragicomedy. Polinesso had dressed Dalinda in her mistress's clothes and had invited Ginevra's lover, Ariodante, to watch in order to persuade him of his lady's unfaithfulness. Taking reality for appearance, he wanders off muttering, "Ho troppo veduto: / felice, se senza occhi io fossi suto!" (V, 58: "I have seen too much: happy if I had been without eyes!"). A witness who thought he saw Ariodante commit suicide erroneously reports this to Ginevra, who continues the tragic litany: "La cagion . . . tutta venía per aver troppo visto" (60: "the whole cause came from having seen too much"). Rinaldo, who has learned everything from Dalinda, completes the illogical sequence by challenging Polinesso to a dubious trial by combat: "Or noi vedrem l'effetto" (86: "Now we will see the effect").

Failure to distinguish between possibility, probability, and certainty is one of the deep themes of the *Furioso* and springs from literary and philosophical conventions of Ariosto's time. When Pinabello retells the marvelous truth of the battle between Gradasso and Ruggiero, he affirms his reliability through the cause and effect we saw above, "io 'l vidi, i' 'l so" ("I know it, I saw it"), but admits that the action "al falso piú ch'al ver si rassimiglia" (II, 54: "resembles falsity more than truth"). His resultant hesitancy to speak further is a reflection of what the narrator feels on a different level. Describing Ruggiero's further exploits, the author confesses, "Se non che pur dubito che manche / credenza al ver c'ha faccia di menzogna, /di piú direi" (XXVI, 22: "If it were not that I utterly fear that truth, which has the face of a lie, lacks belief, I would tell more"), and shrugs responsibility by explaining that his "historical" source, pseudo Turpin, knows himself that he speaks the truth which is so wonderful that readers (Ariosto?) will call him a liar. The terminology used and distinctions made by character and author alike conjure up the doctrinal separation of heroic poetry into biography, epic, and romance. According to Castelvetro, for example, history and poetry are similar but not identical, since the former treats actual occurrences but the latter treats what is probable or possible; since poetry cannot aim at "truth," it must enforce the probable by creating convincing appearances and logical necessity, while history reverses this concern. On a metaphysical level, the preference for appearance over "historicity," like Agramante's fatal "sogna" which leads him to think that he outstrips the French in leaders (XIV, 18), summons one of the most portentous metaphors of the Renaissance.

The motif "life is a dream" occupies too vast proportions in the period to be sketched here in any detail, but is too essential to the nature and concerns of Ariosto's poem to go unmentioned; for it is only in a waking dream, where truth and fantasy are alternately displaced, that the reader's mind can telescope boundless space and his senses and imagination can withstand the impression not only of suspended animation and timelessness, but also of extravagant rapidity of movement in a hallucinated world in which becoming eternally preempts and transcends the stability of being. In the endlessly renewed perspectives of the Chinese-box narrative, men and women in love willingly exchange the limits of reality for the freedom of dream and blend a *Liebestraum* with *Liebestod*. Ruggiero's appearance in the dream of Bradamante prompts her to conclude:

> se 'l dormir mi dà gaudio, e il veggiar guai,
> possa io dormir senza destarmi mai. . . .
> ma s'a tal sonno morte s'assimiglia,
> deh, Morte, or ora chiudimi le ciglia!
>
> [XXXIII, 63–64]

If sleeping gives me happiness and waking sorrows, may I sleep without ever waking . . . but if such sleep is like death, O Death, close my eyes right now.

Naturally, it is Angelica who is the greatest catalyst of such dreams of love and death through her ability to stimulate desire of obtaining her and fear of losing her. When the author says of Ferraú that "gli sparve, come io dico, ella davante, / come fantasma al dipartir del sonno" (XII, 59: "she vanished from him, as I say, like a specter at the departure of sleep"), dreaming and waking are confused, since the Spanish knight continues to move about as in a dream, seeking her by a spring in the ubiquitous forest. At a similar or identical sight, Orlando had earlier superimposed her radiant face on a benevolent nature (VIII, 80) —"Senza pensar che sian l'imagin false / quando per tema o per disio si sogna" (84: "Without thinking that images may be false when one dreams in fear or in desire").[19] Deliverance from love's illusion is appropriately described as a genuine waking, which captures with graceful realism the momentary resonance of mystery following a dreamful sleep.

> Come chi da noioso e grave sonno,
> ove o vedere abominevol forme
> di mostri che non son, né ch'esser ponno,
> o gli par cosa far strana et enorme,
> ancor si maraviglia, poi che donno
> è fatto de' suoi sensi, e che non dorme;
> cosí, poi che fu Orlando d'error tratto,
> restò maraviglioso e stupefatto.
>
> [XXXIX, 58]

As one who after a vexing and serious dream, where he appears either to see abominable forms of monsters which do not or cannot exist, or to do strange and outrageous things, still marvels after his senses are given back to him, and he does not sleep, so, after Orlando was freed from error [his madness], he remained astonished and stupefied.

Neither fantasy nor reality is ever pure.

A point of compromise between the real and the imaginary is the symbolic image that links phenomena to the ideas behind them and to each other by analogies which characters somehow detect and share. This is not the cumbersome allegorical imagery of petrified and unqualified emotions, but rather a commonly shared iconography that invites the observer to contemplate the world's mystery more deeply. Two such related images, among others, are clothing and the veil of truth. Taken at face value, dress can mislead, as in the costumes that confuse the sexes or, like Alcina's perpetual veil, that beautify ugliness. But Bradamante, the most notable lady in travesty, appeals to heraldic symbolism which no one mistakes, as an index to her emotions: "L'abito al suo dolor molto convenne" (XXXII, 47: "the outfit suited her sorrow well"; cf. VII, 53). Conversely, Orlando removes the crest from his shield: "Che come dentro l'animo era in doglia, / cosí imbrunir di fuor vòlse la spoglia" (XIV, 33: "as his soul inside was sad, so he wished to darken his armor outside"). Ruggiero periodically "lieva il velo" from Atlante's shield (X, 109), yet in the early cantos the narrow dimensions of his chivalric code leave him perplexed about the proper use of his weapon. Only when he "arrives" at Logistilla's castle and beholds himself in the reflecting surface of its natural gems does he reach a firm state of awareness. It is the only road open to man if he is ever to know anything or anyone, and lies in the direction of Socratic wisdom, Horatian urbanity, and Thomistic virtue.

> mirando in esse,
> l'uom sin in mezzo all'anima si vede;
> vede suoi vizii e sue virtudi espresse, . . .
> fassi, mirando allo specchio lucente
> se stesso, conoscendosi, prudente.
>
> [X, 59]

Looking into them, man sees right into the midst of his soul; he clearly sees his vices and virtues . . . looking at himself in the luminous mirror, knowing himself, he makes himself prudent.

The story of the Mantuan knight who promises "levarti de la scena i panni" (XLIII, 10: "to remove the curtains from the stage for you") reveals to Rinaldo a limitless truth which is the discovery of his own will and himself.[20]

Loss or discovery of self is one of the poem's sustaining and unifying motifs that takes shape in an artificial paradise of one kind or another. To safeguard his ward, Atlante sends Ruggiero to Alcina's domain, but in the process the paladin's body and soul are almost destroyed by her seductive illusions. Astolfo, an earlier believer in the fool's gold of her *paradiso*, vainly attempts to warn Ruggiero about Alcina's black magic and subsequently does free him by dispelling the illusion and thus destroying the castle of Atlante where the minds of men continue to wander aimlessly. Already a participant in two of the story's most memorable episodes, Astolfo takes the Hippogriff of Atlante, journeys to Hell, to the Earthly Paradise, and on to the Moon in order to retrieve Orlando's sense. Though the latter episodes are more spectacular in their action, they are of a piece with the former in their themes. In Renaissance cosmogony, the moon was the mid-point between earthly mutability and heavenly permanence, but it was also regarded in Pythagorean learning as a "little earth" and the symbol of the changing passions in man's soul. Astolfo's journey, then, unifies some of the story's most widespread themes, and requires serious scrutiny.

CHAPTER 5

That Paradise Called Earthly

(*Orlando Furioso*, XXXIII, 110)

IN canto XXXIII Ariosto abruptly begins the tale of Astolfo's journey from Europe to Asia on the *Ippogrifo* and eventually to the bejewelled and gilded kingdom of Senapo in Ethiopia. That legendary king, "come Lucifer superbo" (109), holds sway over Cairo and the course of the Nile. He had once attempted to storm the gates of Paradise and make war on God, who punished him with the "perpetua notte" of blindness and eternal hunger. Astolfo descends like a redeeming angel and delivers Senapo from his saturnine melancholy and from the harpies that devour his food.

> fuggon l'arpie verso la zona roggia,
> tanto che sono all'altissimo monte
> ove il Nilo ha, se in alcun luogo ha, fonte.
> [XXXIII, 126]

The harpies flee toward the blazing zone until they arrive at the great mountain where the Nile has its source, if it has it anywhere.

Into Hell goes Astolfo, where he imprisons the harpies and meets Lidia, whose pride came "de la beltà ch'a tutti gli occhi piacque" (XXXIV, 15: "from the beauty that pleased all eyes"). From Hell Astolfo climbs the slope to Paradise with its many delights and meets Saint John, Enoch, and Elijah, who give him fruits of Paradise which have been denied to Adam since the first disobedience (60). Astolfo is instructed that he is to be the agent for delivering Orlando from madness, and we learn that it was God who made him mad for three months, as he made Nebuchadnezzer mad for seven years, made him show "nudo il ventre," and "l'intelletto sí gli offusca e tolle, / che non può altrui conoscere, e sé manco" (65: "eclipses and takes away his mind, so much that he cannot recognize anyone else, least of all himself"). From there John and Astolfo proceed to the moon to get Orlando's brains.

Cosmic voyages to the moon have such a long and varied ancestry that it would be erroneous to attribute Ariosto's depository of nonsense to the Florentine moon of Dante alone. More specifically than the mythical flights of Icarus, Phaedrus, Er, and the like, or the pseudo-historical winged flights related by Geoffrey of Monmouth in his *matière de Bretagne*, it is fantasies like Cicero's *Somnium Scipionis*, Plutarch's *De facie in orbe lunare*, and especially Lucian's *Verae historiae* that survived the Italian Middle Ages, enjoyed wide readerships in the Renaissance, and offer sharp parallels to Astolfo's flight to the moon and to Paradise.

In the Middle Ages the *Iter ad Paradisum* was a common type of story, dealing with actual journeys by mortal men to paradise. Among these were the stories of Adam's son, Seth, who brought back seeds from the Tree of Knowledge from which sprang the Cross of Christ, and the *Navigatio Brandani*, in which Saint Brandan embarked on a seven-year voyage, guided by an angel to the Fortunate Islands where he saw Hell and Paradise.[1] Most medieval maps include in the Eastern part of the world a picture of the Terrestrial Paradise, surrounded by a high wall or mountain range and containing within it figures of Adam and Eve, the serpent, the Tree of Life, and the fountain which divides into the four streams that water the world.[2] Ethiopia also fascinated early cartographers. Some of the Beatus maps designate Ethiopia as a country of horrible monsters, precious stones and balsam; "Quivi il balsamo nasce," says Ariosto (XXXIII, 105). But the main interest lay in the mystery of the Nile's headwaters, which pass through this country, because, according to the accepted interpretation of Scripture, the Nile was the same as the Gihon, one of the four rivers of Paradise. From this identification came the designation of Cairo as Babylon. Aside from elaborate decorations featuring Paradise and the Last Judgment, the most pronounced characteristic of these maps is that Jerusalem is shown as the center of the world—a trait that is not found in Roman originals from which they may be copies, like the Hereford *mappa mundi* (ca. 1300). City plans of London, Rome, Acre, Jerusalem, and Paris are immensely enlarged, but the British Isles on circular maps are squashed and misshapen. The purpose of exaggeration was to emphasize the most interesting and significant localities, and Palestine, about which a good deal was known and interest was centered, is shown to be almost as large as the rest of Asia put together. Around Jerusalem Christian cities are marked by red and infidel cities by black to indicate the idolatry and evil that overshadow their gold and riches. Italian Renaissance maps like the Borgia and Este charts continue to show the *peregrinatio in Terram Sanctam,* but they seriously modify Ptolemaic information, or rather correct many of the errors that were rife in the early Renaissance editions of Ptolemy's *Geographia,* and abandon Jerusalem as the world's center. Like Paris (XIV, 104), Jerusalem in the *Furioso* no longer belongs to a *corpus terrarum* that commands the author's unswerving adherence, but rather occupies a focal point in his mind which varies as his interests wander. Now he chides his contemporaries for not recapturing the holy city, now he describes it as a mere geographical site, the confluence of East and West (XVII, 18, 73, 75).

That the subject and point of view of the *Furioso* are indebted to the topology of medieval Journeys to Paradise and at the same time to Renaissance concerns for navigation and exploration is apparent even from a casual reading, for the Renaissance was truly the golden age of geographical discovery. By the time of the last publication of the poem the surface of the known earth had almost doubled, but the world was much larger than Toscanelli and other Italian geographers had imagined; as often happens, however, the very errors of science were fruitful. Navigators had known the seas, but now they had conquered the oceans, and soon learned to know the Antipodes, the deserts, and the tropics. In the *Furioso* author and characters confront these discoveries within the limits of their imagination. The image of the poet finding his way that opens the last canto, "Or, se mi mostra la mia carta il vero" ("Now, if my map shows me the truth"), corresponds to the stance of the poet who, in describing the battle of Paris, glances over at Astolfo beyond Araby in Logistilla's domain who "di lontano accenna" (XV, 9: "signals from afar"), and coincides with the timid seaman's preference for circling the globe on a map of Ptolemy.[3] Bradamante learns that Ullania's lovers will be famous "fin che giri il ciel" ("as long as heaven turns") and that she came from Iceland, called *Isola*

Perduta because "quella marina da pochi naviganti è conosciuta" (XXXII, 55: "that sea is known by few navigators"). Navigational knowledge is operative in Ruggiero's voyage to Africa, but is subordinated to the overriding concern for the caprices of nature and Fortune: the ship flounders under the helmsman's hand, but sails true after he abandons ship (XLI, 23–24). Ruggiero does have momentary access to an elevated vision when he flies to England on the Hippogriff and glimpses purgatory (X, 92), but it is Astolfo who most approaches the raised view of the poet.

After Astolfo calls to the narrator to bring him back, he sets sail with the complementary virtues, Fortitude and Temperance, as his guides, and armed with his magic book and horn. Heading for India, he queries Andronica, who explains the arctics and tropics, the merging of the oceans, and the mysteries of Ethiopia and India, and who sings a paean to the Renaissance quest:

> Ma volgendosi gli anni, io veggio uscire
> da l'estreme contrade di ponente
> nuovi Argonauti e nuovi Tifi, e aprire
> la strada ignota infin al dí presente . . .
> e ritrovar del lungo tratto il fine,
> che questo fa parer dui mar diversi . . .
> ritrovar nuove terre e nuovo mondo . . .
> veggio da dieci cacciar mille, a i regni
> di là da l'India ad Aragon suggetti;
> e veggio i capitan di Carlo quinto,
> dovunque vanno, aver per tutto vinto.
>
> [XV, 21–23]

But as the years revolve, I see new Argonauts and new Tiphyses coming from the farthest countries of the West and opening the road unknown to the present day . . . and finding the end of the area that makes this seem two different seas . . . finding new lands and a new world . . . I see ten chase a thousand and the realms on the other side of India subjected to Aragon; and I see the captains of Charles V, wherever they go, conquering all.[4]

She justifies as God's will the darkness intervening between Augustus and the quattrocento and cinquecento of Astrea newly enthroned, of Cortez and Andrea Doria "col proprio ingegno e proprie forze" (31: "with his own genius and his own forces"). Astolfo leaves his ship to mount Rabican, the horse born of fire and wind and nurtured on air (41), and continues to master the elements. Arriving in Egypt, he captures Caligorante so that pilgrims can travel safely, and kills the necromancer Orrilo by reading the secret of his death in his magic book—a classic victory of white magic over black. Though the action is fabulous, the narrator takes great care to situate it in real time which, however, casts a penumbral light on its own realism; we are told that before the end of Astolfo's battle, night was falling on Egypt but that the sun was still high over the Fortunate Islands (cf. 7).[5] Following his triumph, Astolfo and his group take the rough road to Palestine: "a man destra si volse . . . Potuto avrian pigliar la via mancina, ch'era più dilettevole e più piana" (92–93: "turned to the right . . . They could have taken the road on the left side which was more pleasant and more level"). In the holy city they meet Sansonetto of Mecca, recently converted and encharged with defending Mount Calvary from the Caliph of Egypt. Sansonetto gives the sword of Saint George to Astolfo, and in turn Astolfo gives him Caligorante to assist in his enterprise. After being cleansed of his sins in a monastery, he departs. Demonic magic is put to good use in the episode, but the reader is left to infer that Jerusalem's recapture will depend on a fiction.

The quest motif looms large in Ariosto's fictions, since all searching is but a fluctuation of the same impulse. Quests for the beloved, for terrestrial certainty, for paradise, tell us that all below the moon is subject to change. Viewed by anonymous eyes, Angelica's sudden appearance is thus likened to an epiphany of the moon goddess (I, 52). Unlike the aimless wandering of his cohorts, the crusader Astolfo is sent by Melissa on the "via più sicura" of his unique pilgrimage, and by his own will he elects the "man destra" at the end, combining in this manner knowledge with wisdom. Like Henry the Navigator, he is actuated by scientific curiosity and the desire to propagate the faith. The Temperance and Fortitude that accompany him are the virtues prescribed by Aquinas for avoiding concupiscence and idle curiosity.[6] But the stories he hears along his way to the earthly paradise tell of the failure to avoid improper curiosity. The tales of Senapo's assault on heaven and resultant blindness and Lidia's proud beauty and resultant damnation epitomize the lust of the flesh, lust of the eyes, and the pride of life that derived from man's first transgression in Genesis 3:5–7, and were expounded in I John

2:15–16, where man is cautioned not to love the world or the things of the world. And, in their own secular ways, the "inferma e instabil mente" of other knights-errant who seek fame, but are themselves irresolute and unfaithful, epitomize the same over-reaching. Ariosto's description of Ariodante's mistaken reliance on his eyes, premised on the limitations of free will, is ironic but not accidental: "Altrui vide salire, / salir su l'arbor riserbato, e tutto / essergli tolto il disïato frutto" (V, 64: "He saw another man climbing, climbing up the tree that was reserved, and all the fruit he desired being taken from him"). The drama of Rodomonte unfolds within the dimensions of Genesis and Revelation. He is the grandson of Nimrod, the founder of Babel (Genesis 10), and appears draped in a dragon's skin (Revelation 12). His only weaknesses are his pride and Doralice, whom he loves "piú che gli occhi sui" (XIV, 115: "more than his eyes"). Others see him as "Satanasso (perch'altri esser non puote)" (XVI, 87: "Satan [for he can be none else]"), so it is fitting that his destruction should be likened to the crash of a mine on avaricious seekers of gold and that the closing lines of the poem describing his unregenerate death be taken from Dante's fifth circle of hell, near the fallen angels.

Moreover, Astolfo's ascent of the mountain toward Paradise differs in kind from the nascent Renaissance love of mountaineering:

> al cielo aspsira, e la terra non stima . . .
> e giudica, appo quel, brutto e malvagio,
> e che sia al cielo et a natura in ira
> questo ch'abitian noi fetido mondo:
> tanto è soave quel, chiaro e giocondo
>
> [XXXIV, 48, 52]

He aspires to heaven and does not value earth . . . and judges that the fetid world we live in, compared with this one, is ugly and wicked, and that heaven and nature are angry with it: so much is this one sweet, bright and pleasant.

Alpine expeditions, relatively unimportant before the sixteenth century,[7] and other climbing ventures were essentially motivated by esthetic and scientific concerns. Whereas the ascent of Mont Ventoux allowed Petrarch to obey Augustine's injunction not to admire mountain peaks per se (*Confessions*, X, 8), Bembo's venture up Etna and especially Leonardo's ascent to Monte Rosa allowed for greater understanding of earthly ventures. Like the Ficinian imperative "extra vola" ("fly beyond") and the urge to comprehend "uno prospectu simul omnes" (*Theologia Platonica* I, vi; VI, ii: "all things in a glance"), Astolfo's continued love of soaring brings with it an understanding of his former vanities and a desire to share his possessions (XXII, 26), but Ruggiero, "gustato il piacer ch'avea di gire / cercando il mondo" (X, 72: "when he tasted the pleasure he took in going to explore the world"), forgets his promise to Bradamante.[8] As for Astolfo's kinsman, the poet himself, he too must observe the limits of knowledge and guard against overreaching. The Renaissance commonplace of the poet, seen as the creator and master of his own fictional world and arbiter of its conventions of good and evil, conferred high rank on his genius but at the same time the impulse to create made him all the more subject to human propensities and failings and, in the extreme, to madness. Neo-Platonic *furor poeticus*, divine madness, arrogated to the poet certain vatic and heroic prerogatives, but the ability to soar beyond human bounds drew genius all the closer to the contemplative isolation and imbalance of saturnine melancholy, *solo e pensoso*; and from the association with Saturn in his dual role as creator and destroyer, genius was drawn to Lucifer himself, who saw and desired, aspired and fell. The serpent's promise to Eve that her eyes would be opened and she would be like God, knowing good and evil, could well have come from the conclusion of Ficino's *Theologia platonica*.

Centuries of Church fathers had warned against too hot a pursuit of curiosity about matters unrelated to salvation. From the original Fall from Grace in Genesis, *curiositas* was enlarged in scope to embrace not only the insatiable taste for knowledge, but also the desire to acquire and display possessions delightful to the eyes. Eyes were the inroad to the mind of every son of Adam and endangered travellers on the voyage of life. The most notable and symbolic manifestations of the *iter mensis* were the Crusades and pilgrimages to the Holy Land which, as in the case of the Fourth Crusade, degenerated into sloth and the fascination with exotic countries; like Renaissance voyages, spiritual aspirations gave rise to the discovery of the lands of gold and spices, and pilgrimage became perverted into travel (cf. *I Suppositi*, IV, iii). Alarmed by such prospects, Bernard warned monks to avoid the turmoil of the world and to seek the asylum of monastic stability. We can measure how well placed his uneasiness was by the great sport Ariosto takes in turning friars into necromancers (II, 14) and in describing the descent of the angel Michael in search of Silence, supposedly to be found in monasteries. Instead of Silence, Michael finds Discord, Fraud, and related vices. Fraud is thus portrayed in appearance: "Avea piacevol viso, abito onesto, / un umil volger d'occhi" (XIV, 87: "She had a pleasant face, decent dress, a humble way of turning her eyes aside").

Even sage practitioners of astronomy and astrology failed or refused to distinguish them because they both were considered as aids to assist man in plotting and following his future course of action. Opinion was divided, however, on the efficacy of reading the stars to see into the future. Ficino united magic and astrology into a system embracing spirit and nature, the fate of the individual, and the course of history. On the other hand, Pico found himself in the minority of those who declared that the wonders of the mind are greater than those of the sky, and that *sors animae filia*—fate is the daughter of the soul. Ariosto's satires upbraided men of "debol senso" who try to penetrate the secrets of "il cielo immenso" (VII, 38–48), *Il Negromante* implicitly derides the magician's claim to control sun and stars and the juncture of astronomy and astrology (II, i), and the authorial voice in the *Furioso* is essentially of one mind on these matters and treats them at length. Rinaldo's willingness to blame his "iniquia stella" is really a commentary on his narrow vision before the discovery of his own will (XLII, 36), as the reader eventually learns, but usually the split between ignorance (in the character's mind) and awareness (in the reader's mind) occurs simultaneously. Within this loose definition of irony, we can say that the *Furioso* is of several minds. When we move away from the fool's paradise of Alcina to Logistilla's kingdom of reason, what we immediately learn about it is grammatically set off from what some of her guests eventually learn about it; she built it "senza bisogno de' moti superni / (quel che agli altri impossibile parea)" (X, 63: "without need of heavenly motions [which seemed impossible to the others]"). In the same way, Medoro moves through the ranks of the sleeping French camp, killing anonymous soldiers who, however, are individualized for the reader. Each victim is circumscribed by his own fate and misled in his concept of it. We learn of Alfeo:

> medico e mago e pien d'astrologia:
> ma poco a questa volta gli sovenne;
> anzi gli disse in tutto la bugia.
>
> [XVIII, 174]

Doctor and magician and versed in astrology: but it was of little use to him this time; rather, it told him a lie in everything.

And of Andropono and Conrado, who that day had been lucky at gambling: "Ma non potria negli uomini il destino, / se del futuro ognun fosse indovino" (177: "But fate could do nothing to men if each one could divine the future").

Even in contexts that are ostensibly noncommittal, Ariosto stresses the point that the ineffective blows on Orrilo, who always managed to reconstruct himself, are like the splattering of an alchemist's quicksilver (XV, 70). The happy few who are privileged to witness a portrayal of their future do so not through their own means but through a deus ex machina. Before introducing Bradamante and others to Merlin's hall with its gallery of pictures of Italy's future, Ariosto expressly cautions:

> Ma di saperlo far non si dia vanto
> pittore antico né pittor moderno;
> e ceda pur quest'arte al solo incanto
> del qual trieman gli spirti de lo 'nferno.
>
> [XXXIII, 4]

But let no ancient or modern painter brag about knowing how to do it; and let him surely turn over this art to enchantment alone, at which the spirits in hell tremble.

It is through Melissa that the existence of the gallery and Merlin are originally revealed: "T'insegnerò . . . sí ben la via, che non potresti errare" (III, 63: "I will show you the way so well that you cannot err"), and it is through her constant intercessions that the prophecy of Ferrarese glory is finally initiated through the marriage of Bradamante and Ruggiero: "De l'avvenir presaga, sapea quanta / bontade uscir dovea da la lor pianta"

(XLVI, 76: "She forsaw the future, she knew how much goodness would issue from their line"). Now, Melissa's recurrence in Ariosto's tapestry has puzzled critics. From her earliest to her last appearances, she is a "saggia incantatrice" skillful in exorcizing devils (III, 21), except for her appearance in canto XLIII, which is so anomalous that it requires detailed analysis.

The action really begins in the previous canto when Rinaldo refuses the cup proffered by the Mantuan knight, which would inform him of his wife's fidelity or betrayal.[9] It is against this background that the author preaches against the natural enemy of soaring genius and the cause of its fall:

> O esecrabile Avarizia, o ingorda
> fame d'avere . . .
> Alcun la terra e 'l mare a 'l ciel misura,
> e render sa tutte le cause a pieno
> d'ogni opra, d'ogni effetto di Natura,
> e poggia sí chi'a Dio riguarda in seno;
>
> [1-2]

O execrable Avarice, o voracious hunger of possessing. . . . One man measures the earth and the sea and the sky, and fully reveals the causes of every work, of every effect of Nature, and goes so high that he looks into the bosom of God.

The subject could not be stated in weightier terms—"E questo sol gli preme, / e ponvi ogni salute, ogni sua speme" (2: "and this alone concerns him, and he puts all his salvation and all his hope on it") and the narrator does not resist interjecting his own opinion: "Non è senza cagion s'io me ne doglio: / intendami chi può, che m'intend'io" (5: "It is not without cause if I lament it: let him understand me who can, because I understand myself"). He too was once madly in love, but now has the kind of self-knowledge and awareness of the limits of human aspiration that both Orlando and Rinaldo now have. After a profound silence Rinaldo makes an observation that every lover would do well to heed:

> Pensò, e poi disse: "Ben sarebbe folle
> chi quel che non vorria trovar, cercasse.
> Mia donna è donna, et ogni donna è molle"
>
> [6]

He thought, and then said: "He would surely be mad who would look for what he did not wish to find. My lady is a woman and every woman is pliable."

He expands it to include any potential Faust:

> Potria poco giovare e nuocer molto;
> che 'l tentar qualche volta Idio disdegna.
> Non so s'in questo io mi sia saggio o stolto;
> ma non vo' piú saper, che mi convenga.
> Or questo vin dinanzi mi sia tolto:
> sete no n'ho, né vo' che me ne venga;
> che tal certezza ha Dio piú proibita,
> ch'al primo padre l'arbor de la vita.

[7]

It could profit little and harm much, because attempting sometimes angers God. I do not know if I am wise or foolish in this, but I do not wish to know more than is appropriate for me. Now may this wine be taken away from me: I am not thirsty for it and do not want any of it to come to me, for God has more forbidden such certainty than he did the Tree of Life to our first parent.

In wine may be found truth but this truth cuts both ways. The complexity of this world is different from unchanging Eden, and knowledge of this condition is irrevocable and parallel to eating of the forbidden fruit.

The Mantuan knight agrees to unveil the truth that almost blinded him (10). A learned man once bought a woman, he relates, and had a daughter by her, whom, in order to preserve her from selling her chastity as her mother did, he exposed only to exemplary women; and he selected the Mantuan as her husband when she was so mature "che ne possa l'uom cogliere i frutti" (17: "that a man could gather fruit from her"). They would have lived happily ever after, but for an enchantress who could move the heavens and who had designs on the knight. Melissa, for that was her name, convinced him that only if he put his wife to the test could he be sure of her fidelity. The enchantress gave him a cup that would reveal the truth to him: drinking wine without spilling a drop would attest to his wife's faithfulness, but the converse was also true. She then persuaded him to leave home under false pretense and, transformed into a handsome young man, to ply his wife with jewels. She succumbed to his blandishment, and Melissa revealed the Mantuan's true identity to his startled wife, but instead of asking forgiveness she berated him, ran off to another man, and did live happily ever after. Thus ends the tale of the Mantuan: "Il mio voler cercare oltre alla meta" (45: "my wish to seek beyond the limits"), to which Rinaldo rejoins that "mente via piú salda ancora è spinta / per minor prezzo a far cosa piú brutta" (48: "a much steadier mind is pushed to do an uglier thing for a smaller price"). The moral is that sinning through congenital weakness is venial, but that overreaching is dangerous. As to the Melissa question, her importance to the exposition, peripeties, and denouement of the *Furioso* makes it untenable to hold that in the vast shuffle Ariosto simply forgot he had created two of them with differing attributes.[10]

In case we may have missed the point, Ariosto sends Rinaldo on his way the next day and has him meet a boatman, who tells the following story. A learned judge, Anselmo, married a chaste woman, Argia, who was also loved by Adonio. In trying to win her attention, Adonio spent his entire wealth and went into a seven-year exile, during which time he had the occasion to preserve a serpent from harm. On his return "alla bellezza / che son di riveder sí gli occhi vaghi" (81: to the beauty his eyes are so anxious to see again"), Anselmo was on the point of leaving on a diplomatic mission and pleaded with Argia to remain chaste. To reassure himself, "non resta che piú intender non procuri / e che materia non procacci al pianto" (86: "he does not hesitate to gather more information and to seek matter for sadness"). He consulted an astrologer who did not need his black art to guess that she would be won over by gold. Meanwhile, Adonio met the sprite Manto, which, he learned, is a metamorphosis of the snake he saved, and which close textual analysis shows to be the sprite that once enabled Ricciardetto to deceive Fiordispina (XXV, 62; XLIII, 102). As Melissa did for the Mantuan, she taught Adonio how to dress as a pilgrim, to persuade and tempt, while she assumed the form of a dog (106)—one of the familiar disguises of the devil. The sight of the pilgrim and the dancing dog that shakes jewels and gold from his fur

fece sí, che per veder si mosse. . . .
Gran maraviglia, et indi gran desire
venne alla donna di quel can gentile;
e ne fa per la balia proferire
al cauto peregrin prezzo non vile.

[107, 109]

Moved her to see. . . . A great marvel and then a great desire came to
the lady for that obliging dog; and through the nurse has no mean
price offered to the clever pilgrim.

Finally, her "superbo cor" was won over, and "Adonio lunga-
mente frutto colse" (116: "Adonio gathered fruit for a long
time"). When Anselmo returned, he learned the truth, was con-
sumed with jealousy, and resolved to kill his wife. In seeking
her, he was led through a "folta selva" to a wonderful palace
that dazzled his eye and mind. The palace guard, an Ethiopian
ugly enough "d'attristar, se vi fosse, il paradiso" (135: "to sadden
paradise if he were there"), told him that the palace would be
his if he would submit to sodomy. From her hiding place Argia
saw all and, unlike the first lady, magnanimously consented to
pardon her husband for his greater crime. The final moral seems
to be that, just as there are two (or more) Melissas in the story,
there are various approaches to the various kinds of knowledge
that are available to us throughout life; the greater part of wisdom
may be the realization that we are all subject to error on this side
of paradise.

CHAPTER 6

Perhaps It Was Allowed by God the Avenger

(*Orlando Furioso*, XLII, 5)

SIMULTANEOUS but differing approaches to knowledge that remains forever penultimate have perennially charmed readers of this ironic world, although the nature of its irony has bedeviled generations of critics. Two notable readers of Ariosto, Francesco De Sanctis and Benedetto Croce, have enlarged the scope of his irony to make it coterminal with the total poem, and in so doing have denied the discreteness of characters, ideas, and events. Croce set up a dialectic opposition involving Artistic Harmony that somehow includes but supersedes individual content, while for De Sanctis "reconstructing the past not as reality but as art, at the same time seeing it as a simple game of the imagination or pure art, and pursuing it with its irony, is the inner life of the world of Ariosto." This turns out to mean that "this world . . . is utterly wanting in the seriousness of inner life."[1] Both attitudes tend to equate subtlety in irony with a lesser degree or even an absence of contrast, so that any ambiguity may be viewed as ironic. More recently, critics have rejected this all-engulfing irony and have suggested that Ariosto is not equally ironic at every moment, that the shades of irony are as varied as the spectrum of emotion in the poem. Accentuating the contrastive elements that Croce detected, Attilio Momigliano discussed the resultant equilibrium in which the autonomy of reality and dream, of subjective commitment and objective distance, is not entirely undercut. Seen this way, irony becomes "a harmonizing force, holding the discordant parts of our complex world together in solution."[2]

This awareness of divergent attitudes coexisting in a world of paradox enables us to appreciate not only the shades of affective irony but also the distinctions among the different angles of perspective enjoyed reciprocally or reflexively by individual figures in the story; by the author-narrator toward the dilemma of his creatures, measuring their impercipience by his superior knowledge; or by the reader outside the work, who may share the narrator's ironic insight or may see him as the object of irony. Although he may be the butt of irony, his self-conscious fussiness reflects a genuine desire to discover the truth and his nagging suspicion that the "facts" are not revealing it. The expression "bagnato e molle" ("dripping wet"), used to describe Ariodante after his attempted suicide (VI, 6), and Ruggiero after his near-drowning (XLI, 50), tempers the reader's impression of seriousness, and reduces to the same comic irony dissimilar episodes at opposite ends of the poem. Yet Ariosto's masterful use of *forse* as a pivot between our perception of appearance and reality—"Forse era ver" (I, 56)—subverts clear-cut distinctions among types of irony and its beneficiaries or victims. The author, his characters, and his readers all share in his leering aside on "le parole / che forse alcuno ha già prese a malizia" (XXXV, 77: "the words that someone may have taken in a roguish way"), following Bradamante's expressed desire to test Ruggiero in a joust, but when the two characters face one another, her taunt "perfido Ruggiero" makes her desire "porlo, e forse ove non era sabbia" (XXXVI, 36: "to put him down, and perhaps where there was no sand") rise above sexual banter, and alternate between *eros* and *thanatos*, reflecting our and perhaps her own indecision as to whether she wishes to put him in bed or in the grave.

To contrast the individual content and artistic harmony of a Renaissance work in terms of a Hegelian thesis and synthesis is to commit a critical anachronism of serious proportions, for one of the outstanding characteristics of Renaissance literature is its resilience and ability to juxtapose two truths in precarious tension without trying at all times to correct a false picture of reality by a true one.[3] Synthesis consists in the ability of an author to create a world that may alternately appear absurd or contradictory, or else organized according to the principles of logic and justice, where personages may move with ease in and out of "historical," probable, possible, or impossible situations, depending on the generic convention the author is pursuing at the moment and on our willingness to suspend disbelief in a work of art. The lack of commitment that De Sanctis and Croce sense in Ariosto implies on his part an attitude toward art that must be defined with great care. Far short of a refusal to engage any idea seriously, Ariosto is reluctant to engage any idea with total seriousness from one context to the next to the exclusion of other possibilities. His lack of commitment is evident in the variety of purposes it is made to serve: that of the satirist of warfare or monastic manners, who is anything but uncommitted, or that of the pure ironist, who simply does not express his moral and emotional position, if any. The cold surface of his satiric manner and the fiery depths of moral indignation behind it must be contemplated together in a tension which is never relaxed. This tension is common to all forms of irony and springs from the basic urge of the ironist, which is to perceive between what is expected and what happens (e.g., the forgiveness of Anselmo by Argia), what circumstances seem to be and what they are (Ruggiero in the land of Alcina), what is known and what is not known (Bradamante in disguise), or what is professed and what is performed (Ferraú's promise *detto* and his failure to accomplish its *effetto*). The neutrality of irony appears in its usefulness for expressing equally the comic and tragic responses to these contradictions. The only real response, then, is the refusal to respond as a committed partisan. It leaves the contradictions over which it plays exactly where it found them, more sharply exposed but in no way resolved.

The way in which Ariosto's irony works demonstrates its inherent tendency to sharpen the tensions of experience rather than to remove them. It penetrates to the depths which the surface texture conceals by dwelling on the surface in such a way that, like Angelica, it becomes translucent but not transparent. The reader's special pleasure lies precisely in seeing the two together and in experiencing the tension which their mutual contradiction generates. Verbal irony in the description of Alcina's castle produces this tension by pretending to look only at the surface; and this pretense postulates a fool who will be taken in by it, who will not see that the ironic statement is about the depths as well as the surface. All forms of irony seem to assume the hypothetical existence of someone who knows the secret, the real meaning, and someone else who does not. As a verbal ironist Ariosto simultaneously hopes that there are wise men who will see what he means and assumes that there are fools who will not.

[114]

Perhaps It Was Allowed by God the Avenger

If there does exist a wise man, one who is psychologically attuned to its unique pleasure, he too will need to assume the existence of this hypothetical fool in order to enjoy the irony. Words and deeds often have a meaning in the reader's mind before they take on meaning for the characters. All the way through the experience of Ariostan irony, from the facts that provoke it to the pleasure it provides, there is this tension between two elements, neither of which can be sacrificed if it is to remain irony.

In modern literature the "someone who knows" is often the author who does not care or despairs that his reader may not penetrate his radically personal secret. Our sense of a purposeless and incomprehensibly vast universe threatened some Renaissance thinkers, caught up in their speculations on the origin and purpose of the universe, the impenetrability of the future, the conflicts between reason and emotion, free will and predestination, society and the individual, the absolute and the relative, and, in such matters as warfare and astronomy, conflict between the human and the scientific; the growth of the objective study of man and his enriched knowledge of the universe were fraught with the Faustian danger of going "so high that he looks into the bosom of God." But for the Renaissance poet it was not quite- true, as Goethe said and Croce echoes, that irony raises man "above good and evil." On the contrary, in using the trope *ironia* "the reader's assent is equally the poet's concern, and it is understood that the reader will give it on grounds of some subtlety in the argument, not some sophistication in the arguer." [4] To say that views on Ariostan irony have changed is another way of saying that views on irony have changed.

The subtlety of irony in the *Furioso* is due largely to a mélange of stylistic modes that number among Ariosto's ironic devices. Like his use of allegory, his irony may infiltrate many genres, may provide serious or comic effects, and may serve purposes ranging from sheer escape to moral instruction. Chivalric parody is the most translucent form of ironic mockery: it acts as a lens through which we look at an object or personage familiar to us (and undoubtedly to Ariosto's readers) and see it, at first glance, almost as it is in fact, the pleasure of recognition being followed quickly by the realization that its characteristic features are slightly distorted. The slighter the distortion, the subtler the parody; and the subtler it is, the better, for the hallmark of good parody is its ironically straight-faced imitation of its victim. Verbal irony makes a statement that appears to mean one thing and actually means its opposite; parody offers its victims the compliment of close imitation that is in fact mockery. Both are equally present in Ariosto's exclamation on the "great goodness of the ancient knights."

In its other comic forms irony has a wider range than parody because it can play with ideas as well as with style; and yet, in its most extreme forms, irony observes with amused detachment the *style* of these *ideas*, the way their original thinker thinks, the way the moonstruck Orlando sees Angelica (VIII, 80). Here the inveterate ironist hovers on the verge of parody of the Petrarchan lover, even if he does not use it as a comic device, because he reduces all ideas to styles of thought, all emotions to ways of feeling, thereby disarming their unique claim to his attention. Ariosto's detachment from the ironic spectacle he observes confers an esthetic quality which objectifies the scene of Orlando's pure subjectivity. The curiously irreducible character of his chivalric parody makes it possible to use it intermittently in a large work like the *Furioso*, to combine it with other comic devices, and to sustain it with slight touches as a vein of amusement running through a narrative, without losing or blurring the special comic effect which it provides. The playfulness, if that is indeed what it is, toward the disjunction of Ruggiero's mission and his actions, of the status of *Orlando* and the attribute *Furioso*, implies an attitude of withdrawal which permits intellectual scrutiny without intellectual, moral, or emotional commitment.

Caricature is closely allied to chivalric parody in that it selects the most salient features of an exemplary knight and throws them into relief by simplification and exaggeration, usually to mock but sometimes to make us recognize with amusement someone we respect (Bradamante) or fear (Rodomonte). In both cases we look at them, and what they represent, through the caricature with momentary detachment, and in that moment we may go beyond recognition to the discovery of something new about their face and character. This is akin to the discovery Cervantes made over the long period of writing *Don Quixote*; setting out to make sport of the tales and ballads of knight-errantry, he composed a book more romantically adventurous than the material he parodied. For the artist who draws it, the caricature may be more exploratory than critical. The simplified and distorted treatment of many of the heads which Leonardo scribbled in his notebooks indicates that he was testing through caricature the artistic possibilities of a certain expression or physical type or animal resemblance, concentrating on and accentuating those features which seemed to hint such possibilities. Caricature can explore because it ignores the complexity of the total object and isolates only its relevant images, thus allowing a sharper focus of attention and a greater sweep to fantasy than is possible in a full treatment in a more "serious" work. Fantasy and irony share the deliberate disengagement from life so striking in parody, which may be closer than any other form of irony to the psychic root of all ironic responses. More is involved in this disengagement than the esthetic distance inherent in the experience of all art. In his parti pris Croce overlooked the tacit acknowledgment of the difference between art and life without which art could not be art. The acknowledgment in the case of irony and fantasy is explicit; and they sharpen the difference between art and life into the severance of life from art, into a deliberate withdrawal from the stresses of life which enter so profoundly into such art forms as tragedy and epic.

In disengaging from life, fantasy withdraws into a realm of libidinal fulfillment in which the conflict between fact and desire is momentarily denied. When Orlando discovers the mounting clues of Angelica's attachment to Medoro, his sense of the facts serves only to increase the need to ignore them. For the reader watching him, irony withdraws into an area of intellectual contemplation in which the disparity between fact and illusion is itself the object of contemplation, so that we are not involved in reconciling them. Orlando seeks release from what is fated in his experience, from the frustrations of desire and the contradictions of reason which we cannot escape in life. In irony we master contradictions by exposing them; in fantasy we master frustrations by ignoring them and reconstituting experience arbitrarily, to suit desire. Ariosto so often blends fantasy and irony because in both there is something inconclusive and evasive. Focussing his attention, as he must, on the disparity between what life is and what it ought to be, he has in them tools designed to deal with a similar gulf between things as they are and things as they may be imagined: between fact and illusion in irony, and fact and desire in fantasy. In his fantasy world, it is the narrator that preserves the human perspective and enables us to accept that world imaginatively. He heightens our sense of the fantastic exaggeration he creates and relates by reminding us of the moral and all-too-human perspective we share with him. The extravagant fantasy with which he is sometimes charged is the result precisely of approaching the unfamiliar in an unaffected style or of taking casual metaphors seriously: the poetic mind literally takes flight to the moon to restore the sense of a lunatic. This multiplicity of vision is explicit in the qualifications he imposes on his use of the *Commedia*—"Ora l'alta fantasia, ch'un sentier solo no voul ch'i segua ognor" (XIV, 65: "Now the high fantasy, which does not allow me to follow only one path at all times"). Like Dante's, his fantastic world is coherent enough to strike us as a world and not a chaos, and to make us believe that it has laws even if we do not always understand them. Narrative momentum is provided by the human efforts of Astolfo and Ruggiero, Rinaldo and Orlando, to fathom these laws. After their initial astonishment, perhaps terror, of facing the incomprehensible, they slowly grasp it, reduce it to order, and make sense of it.

I   *Pro bono malum*

The laws that obtain in the *Furioso* and order its chaos vary in magnitude according to the convention they reflect. Like an ironic God naming his creatures, Ariosto assigns characteristics to his personae, as he did in his comedies, which they can appreciate only in retrospect, if at all. Thus, Filandro is destined to become a philanderer (XXI) and Giocondo, "diventò giocondo" when he realizes the trick that has been played on him (XXVIII, 39).[5] Even the formula of imperial investiture pronounced by Charlemagne, "*Este* signori qui" (XLI, 65: "Be sovereigns here") is based on a spurious etymology. In a more serious vein, many episodes illustrate the irony and inherent complexity of life that is implied in the motto *Pro bono malum* (*bad for good*), which Ariosto took for his official seal and which his characters take literally: "'l ben d' uno è il mal de l'altro espresso" (XX, 67: "the good of one is the clear evil of another"). For his good turn in killing the Orca, Orlando suffers the ill will of the villagers he liberated (XI, 48), and Filandro is misled by Gabrina into killing his friend while he was trying to aid him (XXI, 49). Still, a few fortunate souls like Adonio learn that good can come from bad: "Ecco un' alta aventura che lo viene / di sommo male a porre in sommo bene" (XLIII, 77: "Here is a high adventure that comes to take him from the lowest ill to the loftiest good").

The rise and downswing outlined in this passage and the implicit presence of *Aventura* call up the most universally recognized emblem of irony: the wheel of Fortune. Similar passages could be multiplied many times because their theme was of serious moment in Ariosto's age, occurs time and again in Pulci, predominates in the actions of Boiardo's Fata Morgana, and fell within the far-reaching debates over *virtù* and grace, over man's ability to pursue and develop his own native gifts in the shadow of an overriding Divine Providence that predetermines the limits of his success. Men of all conditions defended and attacked the proposition that *virtù* was able to impede the wheels of the goddess Fortuna. The long-standing iconographic tradition attached to Fortuna lent her such clear delineations that she enters battle scenes as a visually active participant (XLVI, 135), although the power she wields and the predisposition of the face behind the mask remain those of *ambigua fortuna*.[6] Within the framework of the antagonism between Cross and Crescent, the workings of God and Fortune coalesce in a fixed manner, as in Dante. Agramante, who can lay no claim to the gift of grace, eventually decides to retreat to Africa, "ma il suo fiero destin che non risponde / a quella intenzïon provida e saggia, / vuol . . ." (XXXIX, 78: "but his proud fate which does not correspond to that thoughtful and wise intention determines . . ."). Conversely, to the French forces "possanza e ardire / piú del solito è lor dato di sopra (che venuto era il tempo di punire / i Saracin)" (82: "More than usual power and boldness is given from above [because the time had come for punishing the Saracens]"). The gifts to the massed French forces are conspicuous for their omissions, and we must observe the distinctions Ariosto makes between collective valor and individual *virtù*, which at times seems to approach sophistry: in a scheme of continual preemption, Fortune and valor can acquire riches (XIV, 56), Fortune can overthrow riches but not individual virtue (III, 37), yet *virtù* needs Fortune to attain success (XVI, 46).

Dedicated to Ippolito d'Este, the conclusion of the poem officiously prefigures his birth: "l'Aventura / l'avea per mano, e inanzi era Virtute" (XLVI, 86: "Fortune had him by the hand and Virtue was present"). This frozen picture, however, is quite different from the dynamic and liberating concept of *virtù* whereby man demonstrates his inner powers and resources in art, statecraft, or warfare, which *Il Principe* claimed were one and the same. The proem to canto XV, "Fu il vincer sempremai laudabil cosa, / vincasi o per fortuna o per ingegno" ("Conquering was always a laudable thing, whether one conquers by fortune or by intelligence"), and the themes that follow it up (31) could well paraphrase chapter headings from Machiavelli's handbook (e.g., "Of New Dominions Acquired by the Power of Others or by Fortune," ch. 7).

With equal conviction characters espouse contrary propositions on "Fortuna, che di noi potea / piú che noi stessi" (XXIII, 30: "Fortune, who could work more on us than we ourselves"), but these contradictions are soluble, or at least apprehensible, when one takes into account changing narrative demands and differences in personality and situation of the principals involved. The last passage is attributable through indirect discourse to Bradamante, who had failed to appear at Vallombrosa in preparation for her marriage. By allowing his heroine to justify her actions in light of "la sua fortuna rea" (XXII, 98: "her evil fortune"), as he had earlier excused Ruggiero's lack of resolve (X, 72), the poet momentarily vindicates his ideological heroes and sanctions his episodic technique. In the preceding canto that technique had deeply involved Ruggiero in its intricacies; going to Vallombrosa for his baptism, he is sidetracked to save Ricciardetto, and in order to accomplish this act of chivalry he must pass through the custom at Pinabello's castle. Far from a blasphemous suggestion of God's indifference, his summation of his situation is cavalier only in that it underlines the code enjoining the knight to ennoble himself through self-reliance and to dedicate himself through action.

> facciàn nui quel che si può far per nui;
> abbia chi regge il ciel cura del resto,
> o la Fortuna, se non tocca a lui.

[XXII, 57]

Let us do that which can be done by us; let him who rules heaven be concerned with the rest, or Fortune, if it is of no concern to him.

But again, natural law in the *Furioso* is subject to the conventions of art. Prior to the disgrace of Martano, who appropriates the rightful glory of others as he appropriated Grifone's armor, we are given to believe in God's will "per mostrar ch'ancor di qua non niega / mercede al bene, et al contrario pena" (XVIII, 77: "to show that even here he does not deny reward to the good and punishment to the opposite"), because this is precisely the way the literal-minded Grifone conceives the world of chivalry and honor. On the other hand, the conclusion of Filandro's tragic murder of his friend—" 'l consiglio del mal va raro invano," (XXI, 48: "the evil man's plan is rarely in vain")[7]—is only a provisional conclusion that piques the reader's suspense and waits to be reversed in a few cantos. Ariosto's use of temporal adverbs here and elsewhere to mitigate categorical statements has the same effect as the contingent *forse*. Just as the *Furioso* unveils the workings of Fortune, who often oversees lunatics (XXX, 15), it speaks guardedly of "Dio, che *spesso* gl'innocenti aiuta" (XXIII, 53; emphasis added: "God, who *often* helps the innocent").

Like Fortune, the ambiguities of nature reflect the predisposition of those, author and character alike, who are beholden to her as a mother or beset by her as a stepmother. To the narrator in his role as woeful lover, nature and fortune are locked in unending struggle (*Capitoli* XI, 53), while as the apologist for the House of Este he can speak of "le grazie inclite e rade / ch'alma Natura, o proprio studio dare, / o benigna Fortuna ad uomo puote" (XXXV, 5: "the illustrious and rare graces which animating Nature or his own study or benevolent Fortune can give to man"). Fiordispina's claim that man

> non potria scioglier quel nodo
> che fece il mastro troppo diligente,
> Natura d'ogni cosa piú possente.
>
> [XXV, 37]

Could not undo that knot tied by the too-careful master, Nature the most powerful of all things,

shares the same ambivalent perspective and is bathed in irony because her lover Ricciardetto goes on to correct the imbalance of "troppo diligente Natura" by means of an artful deception that momentarily satisfies all parties. The most outstanding instance where the author and his creatures participate in the spectacle of nature at odds with art is the first appearance and subsequent uses of the Hippogriff, that marvelous combination of mare, lion, and eagle, which allows the mind to soar beyond its normal limits. Its first mention by Pinabello as "un destriero alato" (II, 37: "a winged horse") is so offhand as to be misleading. When the narrator describes it in earnest he protests that

> Non è finto il destrier, ma naturale,
> ch'una giumenta generò d'un grifo . . .
> Non finzïon d'incanto, come il resto,
> ma vero e natural si vedea questo
>
> [IV, 18–19]

The steed is not feigned, but natural, born by a mare to a griffon . . . This is clearly not a simulation of enchantment, like the rest, but true and natural.

Implicitly supporting Ariosto's contention that the contrivance is natural, modern editors send the reader to Vergil and Pliny, Pulci and Boiardo, to show that the animal is not an original fiction. What is overlooked, however, is that Vergil used the example of crossing griffons and horses to suggest an impossible or grotesque situation, much like the offensive creation that Horace mentions at the beginning of the *Ars poetica*. In the fourth century, Servius, the founder of Vergilian exegesis, commented that griffons hate horses; thereafter the proverbial expression "Jungentur jam grypes equis" ("to breed griffons and horses") became the tag for any incongruity or figment of imagination up through Descartes (*Meditations*, I, III). So when Ariosto claims that his second-generation fantasy is real and natural, we may take him at his word only within the dimensions of an artistic creation where nature may be correctly or improperly used, but where cosmological and esthetic canons that delimit the unnatural are incorporated into the impartial eye with which Nature views high and low.

On such a universal scale, association of Fortune with the three Parcae who regulate man's lifeline equates her hegemony with that of physical nature which precedes and outlasts man (X, 95; XXXIV, 90); but the dual reference of *natura* to human attributes

and to the terrestrial setting in which those attributes are tested
gives the concept a resonance that surpasses the range of meaning
attached to Fortune. After Ruggiero has undergone many trials,
he finally realizes that he has merited all the good "che concede /
Natura al mondo" and by his "proprio studio acquisita" (XLIV,
49: "that Nature grants to the world," "acquired by his own care").
The combination of physical and personal characteristics is both
desirable and necessary for his final test against Rodomonte,
whose evil traits have also been enhanced by the gifts of nature
(XXXVII, 41). As the benefactress of the gifts of the earth,
nature appears as the all-controlling, harmonizing force behind
the ceaseless generation of seasons and seemingly irregular muta-
tion of forms in the world beneath the moon. She is thus greater
than the sum of her parts which, because of her attachment to the
unmoving stars and empyrean, she creates but does not necessarily
love.

We have seen how reliance on classical and medieval conventions of descriptive detail confers the static qualities of dream
and déjà vu on the *locus amoenus*, both in the artful illusion of
Alcina and in the natural creation of Logistilla. Far from these
Arcadian groves, the same sense of uniformity prevails in the
description of battle settings decorated by "un boschetto di
cipressi / che parean d'una stampa tutti impressi" (XXXVI, 41:
"a grove of cypresses which seemed all stamped by one die").
A proverb like "a trovar si vanno gli uomini spesso, e i monti
fermi stanno" (XXIII, 1: "men often go to find one another, and
the mountains stand firm") has both literal meaning and symbolic
weight. The impression created is that of the two-dimensional
surface so characteristic of medieval painting in which rocks,
plants, and buildings are deployed beside or above one another
on one or more standing planes, or freely distributed upon but
not within vast areas of sea and land, and in which trees are
painted uniformly because they are meant to stand for "a forest."
In the *Furioso* figures traverse an appliquéd landscape of similar
embellishments, "un prato / d'arbori antiqui e di bell'ombre
adorno" (II, 34: "a field adorned with antique trees and beautiful
shadows"), where, in this instance, epithets serve to universalize
rather than particularize the scene and reduce it to stasis by
balancing the line of verse. In this scene we are watching Bradamante move between "un culto monticel" ("a cultivated hillock")

and "una valle inculta" ("an uncultivated valley"). This recurring
and recursive movement "per terren culto, o per foresta" (XIII,
54: "through cultivated land or through forest"), between controlled and natural impulses, describes one of the primary
rhythms of the work and of the life of its protagonists, leaving
the reader to feel that the more scenery changes, the more it
remains the same.

But nature is not simply "there." In the *Furioso* it is what it
perhaps always is: a landscape but also a soulscape reflecting
the human microcosm in perspective. Indeed, the flux of sorrow
and laughter, of light and shadow illuminates the meaning and
profound unity of the work only when it is seen in perspective.
And this perspective involves but also transcends individual will
and even mankind—the totality of which is often lost from sight
and disintegrates in kaleidoscopic change—in order to embrace
every impulse of creation. Scenes change to accommodate, mirror,
and ultimately to become seasons of the mind in a fusion and
confusion of man and nature which erases clear lines between the
animate and inanimate. The total fusion of animated nature and
the naturalized features of Olimpia suggest her radiant beauty
that shines through her tears, not as an objective or realistic
observation but as Orlando and Oberto, her future husband, see
her:

> Era il bel viso suo, quale esser suole
> da primavera alcuna volta il cielo,
> quando la pioggia cade, e a un tempo il sole
> si sgombra intorno il nubiloso velo.

[XI, 65]

Her beautiful face was as the sky is sometimes in spring when the
rain falls and at once the sun scatters the cloudy veil around it.[8]

The harmonious vision cannot be isolated from the rhythm of the
incidents that precede it (Orlando engulfed by the furious island-
ers) or that follow it (Orlando emprisoned in Atlante's castle),
because in all three situations he is momentarily captured or
captivated by the forces around him. Between two deeply agitated
stretches in the land of adventure that threaten to annihilate first
his body and then his mind, he is allowed to catch his breath.
Bemused, Orlando stands before this picture of natural charms

and feasts his eyes. In line with the poetic tradition of which Petrarch is one of the great milestones, nature seems to invite or oppose man's actions, according to his emotional predisposition or the will of fate—which may be facets of the same thing. Following her escape from the French camp Angelica approaches a pleasance (which she shortly becomes) with its familiar features "ch'invitano a posar chi s'appresenta" (I, 38: "that invites to pause whoever appears"), conspire to frame her beauty (52), and later the sea pays her court while its breezes seductively tousle her hair (VIII, 36). Yet for others the "mar d'amore" becomes the "empio mar" (XIX, 62: "cruel sea") and the winds that play over Angelica turn on Orlando and devastate the natural beauty around him as a reflection of the storm that rages in his mind (VIII, 81).[9]

II *Outside of Nature's Law*

The "mar d'amore" is a Petrarchan conceit like so many others —like the fire that burns more fiercely inside a log (VI, 27; VIII, 34) or like the nail that drives out another from a timber, just as one emotion displaces its opposite in the mind (XXVIII, 98; XLV, 29)—which all teach the inconstancy of love and at the same time stylize the images of nature they draw on. Owing to the repetition of these stylized images in different contexts, emotions are correspondingly stylized; owning to their vast literary ancestry, the amorous dilemmas of individuals are broadened in scope by the fictional antecedents they conjure up. In chapter 2 we saw that Bradamante's speech in XLIV, 61–65, was lifted verbatim from *Capitoli* XIII and, in the details of its narrative introduction, still bears the marks of that transfer. At one point Bradamante tells Ruggiero that "si vedrà tornar verso la cima / de l'alpe il fiume turbido e sonante" ("one will see the murky and roaring river turn toward the summit of the Alps") before her feelings change. If Ruggiero had witnessed Bradamante's earlier lament in XXXIII, 60, he would have heard her attribute the same words to him; if he had read *Capitoli* XIII, had read Euripides, Ausonius, Cicero, Vergil's first eclogue, Horace of the *Odes*, Ovid of the *Heroides, Metamorphoses,* and *Tristia,* or even Psalm 114, he would have found the same image. Aside from the weight of literary tradition, Ariosto has the deft ability to take proverbial expressions literally, such as that Grifone sleeps "quiet as a mouse" (XVII, 109), and when Astolfo sounds his horn in

Atlante's castle, "not even a mouse" is left behind (XXII, 22). Far from reducing the scene to absurdity, the image caps it, much as the similar comment of the night watch in *Hamlet* (I, i, 10) prepares the awesome appearance of the ghost.[10]

In pursuing these images, Ariosto frequently begins with an unprepossessing allusion, as in the hunting scene during Ruggiero's dissipation when he and Alcina set nets and traps of soft birdlime for "foolish pheasants" (VII, 32). The images of birdlime snares and nets become the commanding metaphors for the trap of love into which most characters fall, but with unequal effects (XLIII, 144). In the stylized flow of these images it is the inequality of effect, the contrast of vehicle and tenor, and the incongruity of image and context that predominate and undermine an absolute adherence to chivalric ideals. Time after time the mad rush of the Saracens is compared to a herd of wild pigs and Rodomonte is likened to a wild boar,[11] comparisons that are wide of the mark in the case of Moslems and not to be taken lightly in view of the contemporary situation in Spain where Moriscos and Maranos were hauled before the Inquisition and tortured, solely for a suspected aversion to eating pork. The religion of the crusaders is not subjected to the same sly irony, but is so secularized that it flows naturally from the pen of the narrator and adapts easily to every context, thus accentuating its distortions. *Vade in pace* (Go in peace), the threnody repeated by the narrator confronted with the spectacle of Isabella's execution, is more an invitation to contemplate the enduring testimony to her fame than the triumph of her risen spirit (XXIX, 27), and the explanation of Aldigiero of Clermont for being unable to rescue Malagigi and Viviano, "l'animo è pronto, ma il potere è zoppo" (XXV, 76) is a clear deformation of Christ's admonition of Matthew 26:41. It could be argued from these examples that the Christian ethic is so pervasive that it touches every phase of human concerns. But the reasons for Ruggiero's refusal to kill Leone, "ordina l'uomo, e Dio dispone" (XLVI, 35: "man proposes and God disposes"), originally formulated by Thomas à Kempis in the *Imitatio Christi*, I, 19, is here more courtly than Christ-like. And the Golden Rule, which is invoked to crown the salacious *novella* of Fiammetta, is couched in the negative, "non far altrui . . ." (XXVIII, 82).

Despite the easiness of Ariosto's manner and his *sprezzatura*,

it would be a mistake to underplay the extent to which an awareness of traditional stylistic casts, one might say formulas, imbues
the *Furioso* and directs the vision that underlies it. One need go
no further than the opening line, "Le donne, i cavallier, l'arme,
gli amori," to find an example of epic *tmesis*—the splitting of
major components in a line to form an *abba* pattern and create a
vast, heroic sweep for the mind's eye. Besides the examples of the
Aeneid and the *Divina Commedia* which are always cited as
parallels to this line, the ancestry of its structure also extends to
the opening of the *Chanson de Roland,* "Charles li reis, nostre
emperedre magnes, / set ans toz pleins . . . ," and recedes back
to or even beyond Horace's *Carmen Saeculare.*[12] With one foot
in this tradition, Ariosto recreates his world, by rearranging its
components, in his own image—an analogy between poetic creativity and divine cosmogony that takes form in countless examples of Renaissance theory and practice.

One of the most intriguing of these notions, theorized by
Cusanus, Ficino, and others, and which in recent years has drawn
the attention of Renaissance scholars, is that the world was
created according to mathematical laws, that numbers constitute
the relative relationship of time and space—indeed, that the creation of numbers equates with the creation of things—and that
man can approximate the mathematical scheme of things in his
understanding or even reproduce it through his own creative
efforts. Transmission of numerological lore from antiquity to the
Renaissance took various circuitous routes that occasionally
crisscrossed and fused. Among these routes were primarily:
biblical allegories and cabalistic exegesis of Scripture; discoveries
of natural philosophy relating to physiological proportion and
visual perspective, typified by Leonardo's sketch on human proportion based on a commentary of Vitruvius, which enabled
observers of natural phenomena to contemplate Platonic ideas
beneath surface appearance; the mélange of occult relationships
attached to Neoplatonism, Pythagoreanism, and astrological in-
vestigation of the cosmic order which were stimulated by an
influx of Arab texts and especially by Ficino's publication of
Hermes Trismegistus; and the literary tradition that drew broadly
on the resultant *silva signorum.* In imaginative literature numerology took the shape of either an organizing principle of the
formal elements of a work (e.g., the books of the *Aeneid,* deriving

from the "beautiful" number twelve) or symbolic value of its action (Charlemagne's struggle lasts for the "perfect" number of seven years), or adapted both number symbolism and formal numerology to its particular ends. Organization of the *Furioso* according to "occult symmetries" has been guardedly alluded to by Giuseppe Toffanin, and would take us far beyond the scope of this book.[13] Number symbolism, however, is more readily apparent.

The number seven figures prominently in the poem, in the light of both its favorable and unfavorable associations. Taken as the sign of earthly mutability, it marks the years of Adonio's exile before his return to his lady in disguise, and the seventh-day metamorphosis of the "diabolic" Melissa, who assists him in his scheme (XLIII, 80, 98). More favorably, the number seven, as in Dante and scholasticism generally, is the sign of universality and the very image of man. Marfisa came into her majority, so she explains to Charlemagne, by capturing seven kingdoms (XXXVIII, 15), and her brother Ruggiero, just before his baptism, forced Dudone to free seven captive African kings (XLI, 6). Now, despite the long-standing views on Ariostan irony which some would stretch to include cynicism, it is difficult to overlook the seriousness and ceremony with which such numbers are set forth. Moreover, as we have suggested, however darkly his irony may at times be colored, it need not exclude a respectful nod or a sly wink at contemporary attitudes toward numerology and the chivalric traditions according to which knights had to undergo rites of trial and purgation on the way to worthiness. With no suggestion of levity—except for the irony of the lunar landscape that surrounds him—Saint John explains to Astolfo that Orlando, unlike Nebuchadnezzar with his seven-year madness, must wander for only three months, reminding us that three is the symbol of cosmic peace and harmony (XXXIV, 66). Accordingly, we read later when he restores Orlando's sense that

> Lo fa lavar Astolfo sette volte,
> e sette volte sotto acqua l'attuffa;
> sí che dal viso e da le membra stolte
> leva la brutta rugine e la muffa
>
> [XXXIX, 56]

Astolfo has him bathed seven times, and seven times immerses him in the water; so that he removes the slime and scum from the madman's face and limbs.[14]

Ruggiero's baptism is performed by a Christological figure who has been in exile for forty years and who knows that Ruggiero must die seven years from the day of his conversion, a death which prepares his transfiguration in the Este line.

Aside from symbolic accretions to these specific well-chosen numbers, knights are made to move easily among multiples of one hundred or one thousand as a way of enhancing the epic expansiveness and awe that surrounds them. Three hundred is the number invoked to suggest splendid pageantry and heroic deeds much as Vergil uses *ter centum* and *sex centum* to express vague exaggeration.[15] At one more remove, Ruggiero's three-thousand-mile trip from France to Alcina's island (VII, 25) should not be taken literally, as it has been by numerous puzzled commentators, any more than the six thousand Amazons in XIX, 65. Rather than calibrating exact space and time, then, elementary and round numbers suggest magnitude and general or circumscribed meaning and values which may vary in their reference as context varies. Thus, the figure *mille* is used randomly to intimate the expansiveness of war and love (XXXI, 60); to convey the idea that, just as the reign of a good monarch lasts seven hundred years, so any pleasance looks to a millennial future, "ch'in mille anni o mai più non è raggiunto" (I, 48: "which is not again encountered in a thousand years or ever"), and to sanctify the armor of Homer who has been dead for a thousand years (XXIII, 78). The "boundary" number *one thousand* is invested with unifying attributes which in these instances become progressively specific in reference and meaning. In the last case, the number is appropriate, as no other number would be, because one thousand years was the supposed duration of each of the seven ages of man; it was derived from prophetic myths about the Christian millennium—a time when, after a cosmic battle between Christ and Antichrist, the forces of evil are locked away forever, the dialectic of history is abolished, and a reign of permanent, static harmony prevails over the earth. Similarly, seven hundred is the number of men attributed by Ariosto to Ruggiero in deference to the established Italian tradition (XXXI, 65), but in other contexts Ariosto assigns to it a reference and resonance that particularly interested him; it measures the distance from the time of the story to the time of the narrator, as Merlin foresaw it—"fra settecento anni vi saranno, / con grande onor del secolo futuro" (XXVI, 39: "in seven hundred years they will be here with great honor of the future age"), and interests a personage like Rinaldo, who is not gifted with prophecy, as an invitation to contemplate some vague golden age:

> udí da Malagigi, il qual seco era,
> che settecento volte che si sia
> girata col monton la quarta sfera,
> questa la piú ioconda isola fia
> di quante cinga mar, stagno o riviera
>
> [XLIII, 57]

He heard from Malagigi, who was with him, that when the fourth sphere will have turned seven hundred times with the ram, this will be the most delightful island of those encircled by sea, lake, or river.

III *By Long Experience Taught*

Organization of action in the *Furioso* according to certain fixed numbers aligns it with the epic and romance works from which it partly springs and guides its protagonists to the realization of their manifest destiny. The numbers that delimit a hero's thought and action are ambivalent in that the aggregate of meaning ascribed to them is in flux, and in that they define simultaneously the vastness and limitations of his power. Numerical ordering in the propitiatory rites the paladins accomplish is analogous to the limits of truth and illusion which they must learn; both are part of the initiation, education, and preparation that constitute one of the basic rhythms of this and many other chivalric romances. Astolfo, and Ruggiero after him, must learn the true proportions of the Alcinas of this world (VII, 15, 73) before they become worthy of receiving and executing the missions given to them, just as, let us say, Spenser's Red Cross Knight begins in innocence and must commit momentous errors before attaining perfection. Bradamante, too, is initially described as a balance of innocence and potential, "che come era animosa, / cosí mal cauta" (II, 74: "as lively as she was incautious"), and this absence of preconceptions and her resultant attitude of humble receptivity—"Di che merito son io, / ch'antiveggian profeti il venir mio?" (III, 13:

"Of what merit am I that prophets foresee my coming?")—make her ideally suited to benefit from the experiences she undergoes.

Knowledge of their illustrious ancestors and glorious progeny responds to the eulogistic end of the poem and helps to resolve many of the dilemmas that perpetually confront Bradamante and Ruggiero (e.g., XXXVI, 70–71). Ruggiero benefits from being thrust into the company of mentors graced with the Horatian traits of *ratio atque usus, virtus et sapientia*, such as the ferryman, "saggio e di lunga esperïenza dotto" (X, 44: "wise and taught by long experience"), who applauds his escape from Alcina's wiles. Yet, as we have suggested, Ariosto conspires to accentuate his imperfections, making him fickle and obtuse, leaving the stout-hearted Bradamante bereft of hope—"Poi ch'in questo ancor manca, non le avanza / in ch'ella debba piú metter speranza" (XLII, 24: "Since he is also lacking in this, she is left nothing in which she can place her hope any more")—prolonging suspense, and creating momentary imbalances in the narrative line which last until the final octaves of the work: "Ruggiero, ancor ch'a par di Bradamante / non se sia dotto, pur gli torna a mente . . ." (XLVI, 99: "Ruggiero, although he was not instructed in them [the cryptic prophecies of Este greatness] as well as Bradamante, still he remembers . . ."). As the poem prepares for its denouement in canto XXXVI, Ariosto skillfully plays off both Marfisa's resolute decision to convert to Christianity (78) and Bradamante's dithyrambic praise of her lover's parentage (79) against the intricate confusion of the following octaves that reel, not with Ruggiero's emotion, but with the plodding turns of his irresolution. The ineluctable rhythm of "di qua, di lá" claims his thought in its movement from one conjunction to another as he searches for the decision that will bring him less dishonor:

> Ruggiero accortamente le rispose
> che da principio questo far dovea;
> ma per non bene aver note le cose,
> come ebbe poi, tardato troppo avea.
> Ora, essendo Agramante che gli pose
> la spada al fianco, farebbe opra rea
> dandogli morte, e saria traditore;
> che già tolto l'avea per suo signore.
> Ben, come a Bradamante già promesse, . . .
>
> [80–81]

Ruggiero shrewdly answered her that he should have done this at the beginning, but for not having known things properly, as he did later, he had waited too long. Now, since it was Agramante who had placed the sword at his side, it would be a wicked thing to cause his death, and he would be a traitor since he had already taken him as his lord. But, as he already promised Bradamante . . .

Ruggiero has become lost in the vast complexity of the work and, like Astolfo abandoned in the far reaches of Araby, must be rescued by his creator.

Representatives of the entire world of knight-errantry, even those that figure most prominently in the poem, are always just offstage. Although the narrator describes them ranging over continents and says they may be subject to Fortune's whim, they are standing in the wings at all times, ready at his beck and call to reenter the flow of action, or, as with Astolfo, demand reentry. The pattern in the narrative fabric that results from their alternate appearance and disappearance is barely symmetrical and perhaps not occult; but it does reflect on the central themes of the work, creates compositional symmetries between *novelle* and the main action, and establishes common cause among the leading players. Ruggiero's conversion and baptism at the hands of the hermit in forty-year exile is prefigured by his near-drowning—"or si battezzi in queste amare e salse" (XLI, 47: "now he is baptized in this which is bitter and briny")—and his wishes to placate God—"ch'ivi punir non lo volesse, / pentito disse quattro volte e diece" (XLI, 48: "so that he would not wish to punish him here, he said that he repented four times and ten"). It would have been further prefigured, for anyone who had access to the forty-six canto structure of the poem, by the near-drowning of the repentent Ariodante who, like Ruggiero, emerged from the sea "dripping wet" (VI, 6). Ariodante's attempted suicide and Ruggiero's new life are both motivated by a consuming love, are situated equidistantly from their respective ends of the poem, and thus are located at an equal distance from the exact middle of the poem where the narrator discourses on the madness of Orlando and of all men. Orlando is centralized because he is the exemplar of all those who suffer love's madness, including himself. Therefore, he is presented as a shadow of his former self in an image that has a visual as well as a symbolic impact:

Non son, non sono io quel che paio in viso: . . .
Io son lo spirto suo da lui diviso,
ch'in questo inferno tormentandosi erra,
acciò con l'ombra sia, che sola avanza,
esempio a chi in Amor pone speranza.

[XXIII, 128]

I am not, I am not the one I appear in aspect . . . I am his spirit
separated from him, which wanders tortured in this hell, so that with
my specter which alone remains, I may be an example to whoever
puts his hope in Love.

His madness, in turn, is fleetingly prefigured:

Ma non vi giunser prima, ch'un uom pazzo
giacer trovaro in su l'estreme arene,
che, come porco, di loto e di guazzo
tutto era brutto e volto e petto e schene

[XIX, 42]

But before getting there, they met a madman lying at the edge of the
sand, all dirty as a pig with mire and sludge on his face and chest and
back.

It is postfigured as well in unrelated episodes, shortly after the
narrator's revelation of the efforts of love (XXIV, 1–2). This
episodic progression and juxtaposition inclines us to have compassion for lesser mortals.

Amore ha volto sottosopra spesso
senno piú saldo che non ha costui,
et ha condotto a via maggiore eccesso
di questo, ch'oltraggiato ha tutti nui.
Ad Odorico debbe esser rimesso . . .

[XXIV, 39]

Love has often overturned a sounder mind than this man has, and has
led to a much greater excess than this which has outraged all of us.
Odorico should be forgiven . . .

Even Astolfo, the opposite of Orlando in his customary detachment, commits a similar error (which anticipates an event in the
Cinque Canti [IV, 54–74]):

Astolfo lungo tempo saggio visse;
ma ch'uno error che fece poi, fu quello
ch'un'altra volta gli levò il cervello.

[XXXIV, 86]

Astolfo lived wise a long time, but an error he made afterwards was what once again took away his brains.

In the *Furioso* he resurrects and reunites the count's mind and assists the cause of Christendom just as Orlando does later (XLII, 1). The only person in the story who attains the outsized status of Orlando, Rodomonte, resembles him in the insane jealousy they both experience after we witness their incredible exploits, and, like Orlando, inadvertently imperils those he is purported to shelter.[16] Relationships among characters become increasingly complex when we pass to other dramatis personae: Charlemagne and Agramante, in their roles ordained by chivalric tradition, occupy similarly distant backgrounds as fatally different antagonists; Doralice and Isabella momentarily occupy the foreground as studies in sentimental opposites, and so on.

Over the years critics of the *Furioso* have pointed out the lack of clear and sustained delineation in its creatures and the patina of individual features and names that often betrays a sameness and paucity of substance beneath the surface. These common features have been attributed to the tastes of the audience for which Ariosto was writing, to the burden of tradition which led him to find genealogies for his characters in literary typologies, to the weight of ideas certain characters are made to bear, and to the changing nature of the poem as it evolved over its vast length. One further reason could be advanced, not necessarily contradicting any of those just mentioned, to explain the impression that true "individuality" is lacking among the cast of characters. It is that the fate of the characters is closely bound up with the narrator, who at times moves among them as one of them and at other times so clearly directs their comings and goings. Even when protagonists find others whose inclinations correspond to their own, their meeting sets up counterpoints with preceding or following episodes. Such is the case with the freeing of Angelica from the Orca by Ruggiero in canto X and the corresponding liberation of Olimpia by Orlando in the following canto. We have seen that both events grew from the same creative impulse on

Ariosto's part. But the mutually sensuous delight of Ruggiero and Angelica, who both forget their absent lovers, and the insistence on mutual continence in the incident involving Olimpia and Orlando, establish the kind of chiastic grouping we have seen elsewhere; here the reversal in motivation runs counter to the parallel structure, emphasizing once again that man wanders through life at odds with his calling and with himself. As it does with Ruggiero and Orlando, contrapuntal perspective marks the activities of Angelica before and after her rescue. Prior to her deliverance by Ruggiero, the narrator laments the indignities that beset her in canto VIII, yet seems to relish relating them. Later, at a point where Bradamante has long since replaced her as the poem's heroine, her marriage to Medoro is portrayed unfavorably:

> molto gli disuase Malagigi
> di piú Angelica amar, che s'era posta
> d'un vilissimo barbaro ai servigi
>
> [XLII, 39]

Malagigi tried hard to dissuade him from loving Angelica any more, who had placed herself in the service of a very lowly barbarian.

Disapprobation, however, must be placed in the perspective of Malagigi's rhetorical end of dissuading Rinaldo from dwelling on her, just as criticism of ladies marrying beneath their class in *I Suppositi* (I, i) must be placed in the context of the social commentary of New Comedy.

Allegorical commentators like Fornari and others have been perplexed by Angelica's inconstancy, because if her marriage is taken as the humiliation and just punishment of pride, it is hard to know what to do with the ennobled example of Medoro, whose character, leading up to his betrothal, is drawn along Vergilian lines.[17] The point is not that Angelica has fallen from grace, but rather that she is no less regal for celebrating her love in the hut of a "cortese pastor" (XIX, 25), and Medoro is no less noble for his humble birth. Their union captures the interplay of light and shadow that always accompanies her in one way or another, because it describes her and because she is all things to all men—shadow to Malagigi and light to Medoro. If we are to speak of descent in this episode, we must respect the imagery and motifs in which Ariosto casts it. It is significant, then, that Medoro's prayer for divine assistance immediately introduces an authorial allusion to the myth of Endymion (XVIII, 185), the love story of the moon goddess for a beautiful mortal to whom was granted perpetual youth and a sleep of dreams in which all things are possible.

CHAPTER 7

Pure and Sweet Speech

(*Orlando Furioso*, XLVI, 15)

IN comparing the Renaissance artist to God on the basis of his superior powers which enabled him to create in his works a generalized humanity or a superior nature, philosophers and poets delighted in refashioning the opening verses of the gospel according to Saint John. Since the word is in the poet and God is in the Word from which all things proceed into existence and by which light illuminates shadowy substance, by analogy the poet became an enlightened seeker able to transcend a world of accident and seize upon the true revelation of things. Ability to transcend creation, however, need not—and in Ariosto's case, does not—extend to the characters in the fictional world. In the *Furioso* they are subordinated to the situations where they find themselves, to the metaphors and figures of speech that join them together when these are used by the poet as the structure of vision, and to the larger patterns of the poem.[1]

The feel of the reader's memory enables him to identify and thus recreate the fictional origin of certain speeches, and the very characters are aware that others and they themselves are not speaking but rather making speeches. As a result, their thoughts and actions become reduced to a literary existence, to "high words that bear semblance of worth, not substance," as Milton said of another rival of creation. Speeches among both Christians and Saracens tend to fall into one of the three traditional fields of rhetoric: the council of war among Agramante, Marsilio, and Sobrino is a classic example of deliberative address to an assembly in which the expediency of a proposal for future action is weighed and discussed (XXXVIII, 37–65); Saint John's encomium to the House of Este conforms in detail to the categories of panegyric, commemorating past or present heroic exploits (XXXV, 9); Bradamante's speech at the Castle of Tristano on the subject "which of two ladies is the more beautiful"—in itself a familiar theme of medieval and Renaissance courtly debate—abides by the rules of judicial address to a court of justice. In this last scene, for instance, her parenthetical remarks and her summation—

> Io ch'a difender questa causa toglio,
> dico . . .
> sarò per sostenergli a suo piacere,
> che 'l mio sia vero, e falso il suo parere.
>
> [XXXII, 102, 106]

I, who undertake to defend this case, say . . . I will be ready to uphold against him that my judgment is true and his is false—

make it clear that she is aware of the role she is playing, of the *Sic aut Non* forensic terminology she uses, all of which resembles the suasory technique used by other characters in other contexts (cf. XLV, 105).

Speech is well chosen for the occasion at hand, and thus determines relationships among characters and the actions they take. When Orlando and Isabella travel in silence, time slips by quickly without any corresponding action: "Senza trovar cosa che degna sia / d'istoria, molti giorni insieme andaro" (XIII, 44: "Without finding anything worthy of telling, they went along together for many days"); but a few stanzas later Bradamante and Melissa revert to the remedy for boredom proposed by the experienced travellers of Chaucer and Boccaccio, "cercando allevïarle tuttavia / con parlar grato la noiosa via" (54: "trying the whole time to lighten the difficult way with pleasant speech"), which gives Melissa the opportunity during the ensuing twenty stanzas to foretell the coming greatness of Ferrara. Despite the length of such speeches, the reader has no right to protest against them because it is the fictional listeners who have requested them and it is they who are spellbound by them. In these scenes it is clear that Ariosto has learned his lesson well from the *Aeneid*, in which the Trojan hero begs the Cumoean Sibyl to utter her long prophecy, and from the *Commedia*, in which Dante frequently requests clarification from his guides on the events he witnesses. Rinaldo is apparently not weary from the long story told by the Mantuan knight, since he requests another tale from the boatman he meets shortly after and settles in for a long narration, giving us our cue to do the same: "Sï che di' pur, se non t'incresce il dire; / che volentieri io mi t'acconcio a udire" (XLIII, 71: "so speak more, if speaking does not cause you regret, because I will willingly settle myself to hear you").

Before the boatman even opened his mouth, Rinaldo was led to attribute certain forensic qualities to the man merely on the basis of his bearing:

> perché di veder tutto il pensiero
> che l'occupava tanto, gli fu aviso,
> come uom che ben parlava et avea ardire,
> a seco ragionar lo fece uscire.
>
> [XLIII, 67]

Since it seemed to him that he saw all the thought that was occupying him so much, as a man who spoke well and had courage, he brought him to the verge of conversing with him.

Here and elsewhere speech is taken as an attribute of mind and soul in both minor and major characters alike, which they recognize and value at sight. Correspondingly, the inability to speak well is a personal detraction equalled only by the inability to fight well or with courage (XLI, 45). A distraught Isabella is dissuaded by a hermit, appearing from nowhere, "who was able to speak so well." The anomaly of a hermit gifted at public speaking is readily explained by the divine inspiration that grips him and the elevated texts he deals in:

> di buoni esempi ornato e d'eloquenzia,
> alla giovan dolente persuade
> con ragioni efficaci pazïenzia;
> et inanzi le puon, come uno specchio,
> donne del Testamento e nuovo e vecchio.
>
> [XXIV, 88]

Adorned with good examples and eloquence, with fitting arguments he wins over the sorrowing maid to patience, putting before her, as a mirror, ladies of both the Old and New Testaments.

On the other hand, the story's ideological hero, pulled between his obligation to Bradamante and his allegiance to his Saracen lord, is steadfastly concerned about the opinion others may hold of him, and so his speech smacks more of artfulness than natural inspiration:

> indi lo priega (e lo fa con bella arte)
> che saluti in suo nome la sorella;
> e questo cosí ben gli venne detto,
> che né a lui diè né agli altri alcun sospetto.
>
> [XXVI, 135]

Then he implores him [Ricciardetto]—and does it with fine artfulness —to greet his sister in his name; and he said this so well that it gave no suspicion to him or to the others.

In the Saracen camp it is the "piú efficaci detti" of the noble Sobrino that win out over the "detti accorti" of Marsilio, thus precipitating the fierce clash on the Isle of Lipadusa near the end of the poem. And it is through the oratorical skill of Leone, "il qual sapea molto ben dire" (XLVI, 61: "who knew how to speak very well") that the culminating marriage of Ruggiero and Bradamante is resolved:

> Rivolse poi con sí efficaci preghi
> le sue parole all' ostinato Amone,
> che non sol che lo muova, che lo pieghi,
> che lo faccia mutar d'opinïone;
> ma fa ch'egli in persona andar non nieghi
> e supplicar Ruggier che gli perdone
>
> [XLVI, 64]

Then he turned his words to the obstinate Amone with such effective entreaties that not only does he move him, implore him, make him change his mind, but makes him not refuse to go in person to Ruggiero and beg his pardon.[2]

In line with the triple purpose of oratory to teach, please, and move, it is appropriate in this last scene that Amone be enlightened, moved to sorrow and to secure the undying happiness of all those present. Emotion is a concomitant of effective speech on the part both of those who listen and those who speak. Bradamante and other abandoned ladies follow the lead of Ovid's heroines in the *Heroides* in speaking through their tears and attempting to move the elements or an anonymous audience to sympathize with their plight (X, 21, 31). Doralice speaks so

well to Mandricardo that "non pur lui mutato di proposto, /
ma di luogo avria mossa una colonna" (XXX, 43: "not only
would she have changed his mind, but would have moved a
column from its place"), and, pleading with Rodomonte to spare
Brandimarte, Fiordiligi "seppe sí ben dir, ch'ancor che fosse /
sí crudo il re pagan, pur lo commosse" (XXXI, 74: "knew how
to speak so well that, although the pagan king was so cruel, still
she moved him"). Yet, like the emotion that controls it, like the
visual aspect by which a listener judges a speaker's veracity, and
like reality itself, the spoken word can be ambiguous and decep-
tive. Rodomonte realizes this after listening to a story in dispraise
of womankind: "Se 'l Valerio tuo disse altrimente, / disse per
ira, e non per quel che sente" (XXVIII, 78: "if your Valerio spoke
otherwise, he spoke in anger and not what he feels"). Is Rodomonte in a position to judge? After all, he is speaking out of the
anger that proceeds from his lovesickness. Moreover, he might
have made the same reproof to the narrator himself, who seems at
times to pretend anger in his defense of ill-treated women. The
reader is ever aware of the author-narrator's hand in stage-manag-
ing these speeches and adapting them to his own ends. At one
point he shifts his glance to Bradamante, "veggiàn che fa quella
fedele amante," who upbraids Melissa and her "mendace suasïon"
for leading her into the sea of love (XLII, 26). Lying which is
here imputed to the truthful and prophetic Melissa sets up her
opposition in the *novella* of the following canto to the deceitful
Melissa, who seems to speak truthfully.

Similarly, it is only the narrator, and the reader with him, who
watches the benign duplicity of Ippalca. Encharged by Bradamante with taking Frontino to Ruggiero—and in fact invented by
the narrator expressly for this occasion—Ippalca meets Rodomonte, who eyes the horse and decides to expropriate it precisely
because it belongs to Ruggiero. Feebly resisting the theft, Ippalca
goads on the Moor by singing Ruggiero's praises, in whom he too
recognizes a "sí gran campion" (XXIII, 35) and concludes:

> Che Rodomonte io sono, hai da narrarli,
> e che, se pur vorrà meco battaglia,
> mi troverà; ch'ovunque io vada o stia,
> mi fa sempre apparir la luce mia.

[36]

You must tell him that I am Rodomonte, and, if he should wish battle with me, he will find me; since wherever I go or remain my light always reveals me.

When she relays this information to Ruggiero, she omits any reference to Rodomonte's praise for his adversary and on the other hand accentuates the Moor's audacity. Hearing this embellished discourse, Ruggiero's hostile reaction is inevitable, as is the life-and-death conflict they engage in twenty cantos later.

I   *Declaimed by a Public Crier*

If the figures in the poem lead a wordy existence and, like Astolfo, may be periodically conscious of the bond to their creator, it is also true that the verbal master who oversees the work is aware of the popular and erudite narrative tradition behind him which delimits the material of his poetry and the concept that he entertains of his role as poet. Application of the techniques of the *cantastorie* to the *Furioso* and the role the fictional narrator creates for himself as one of those wandering minstrels are mutually reinforcing and cannot be easily separated. It is a measure of Ariosto's success in cultivating this role that his own lyrics were pillaged, altered, and sung by *cantimbanchi* throughout Northern Italy after his death. He draws on familiar narrative techniques to establish conventional chronology ("At that time . . . ," "There once was . . .") and conventional settings for action, such as having characters leave or return to their native village (XLIII, 77) according to a pattern that may work to their individual disadvantage but obviously works to the advantage of the narrative itself.[3] At other times he seems to place himself above his work in order better to control its narrative strands, as the inclusion of *novelle* in later editions would seem to require, or else renounces modulating his speech to accommodate the struggling reader—attitudes that are paralleled both before and after Ariosto's example: [4]

> Signor, far mi convien come fa il buono
> sonator sopra il suo instrumento arguto,
> che spesso muta corda, e varia suono,
> ricercando ora il grave, ora l'acuto.
> Mentre a dir di Rinaldo attento sono,
> d'Angelica gentil m'è sovenuto, . . .

[VIII, 29]

Pure and Sweet Speech

My lord, I should do as the good musician does on his fine instrument, for he often shifts his cord and varies his sound, now seeking the grave, now the witty. While I have been concerned with speaking of Rinaldo, I remembered Angelica.

> intendami chi può, che m'intend'io.
> Né però di proposito mi toglio,
> né la materia del mio canto oblio;
> ma non piú a quel c'ho detto, adattar voglio,
> ch'a quel ch'io v'ho da dire, il parlar mio.
>
> [XLIII, 5]

Let him understand me who can, because I understand myself. However, I am not digressing, nor am I neglecting the matter of my canto; but I do not wish to adapt my speech any more to what I have said than to what I am going to tell you.

However superior or indifferent the narrator may at times claim to be, he remains mindful of the Vergilian model he follows and occasionally likens himself to Dante and especially—by example—to Boiardo. Analogues to the preludes of certain cantos may be found in Claudian, and Ariosto's acknowledgment of an audience grown weary at the end of various cantos is all in the best tradition of the *cantastorie* (e.g., X, 115; XIII, 80); but more pointed comparisons may be drawn with Boiardo, who excels at both of these techniques of asides addressed to the listener. Both Boiardo and Ariosto allege that they found much of their matter in the popular *Historia Caroli Magni et Rotholandi* (ca. 1150). Over a patina of historical legend and compiled chronicles, the presumed author(s) of this work, designated as pseudo Turpin because of the plurality of authorship critics have seen in it, superimposes a world of chivalric romance in which Roland is seen for the first time as a ladies' man. Ariosto moves comfortably within this atmosphere of fact overridden by fantasy, at times citing Turpin as the unimpeachable source of a wild exaggeration, at other times dismissing the inadequate Turpin in favor of some unnamed chronicler (XXIV, 44–45). The ruse allows Ariosto to identify himself with a long-standing tradition, while reinterpreting and expanding that tradition in order to make room for his own artistry.

But it is mainly through his close identification with Boiardo and through his unobtrusive integration into the *Furioso* of material he found in the *Innamorato* that we see his artistic mastery of sources. Assuming that his readers already possess the requisite background, Boiardo barely takes the time to explain that Orlando, "who is enchanted," cannot be wounded (I, iv, 3; I, xix, 4). Ariosto, also brushing aside a labored explanation that his learned audience does not need, goes out of his way to chide the unlettered rabble, "quella gente pazza" (XI, 50), and thus distinguishes the knight's superior qualities all the more. In canto XXXI he augments the mystery of Malagigi's devilish tricks by situating them in the dark of night (86), whereas Boiardo's Malagise had operated in the ill-defined and ineffectual time of *Mentre che* (II, xxii, 50). A few stanzas later Ariosto seems to remember his source—"(credo ch'altrove voi l'abbiate letto)" (91: "[I believe you have read it somewhere else]")—and goes on to abridge "la vera istoria di Turpin" which Boiardo carefully set forth at the beginning of his poem. The end of Boiardo's poem is inserted into the narrative of Ricciardetto, who edits the text (which he could not have read) by excluding all matter not pertinent to the *Furioso* (e.g., the pretext used by Fiordispina to confront Bradamante alone, which closes the *Innamorato*) and to elaborate dramatically all details that bear on the needs of Ariosto's story (XXV, 22–70). In all of this editing and emending of Boiardo's work, Ariosto's control of narrative devices appears clearly between the lines of his text. Through Ricciardetto's speech the author says coyly to Ruggiero—and to readers of the *Innamorato*—"Che voi m'abbiate visto esser potria / (rispose quel), che non so dove o quando" (XXV, 22: "It is possible that you may have seen me [the other answered], but I do not know where or when"). If the reader finds the speech too long, he need only remember that it is made for Ruggiero, who has anxiously requested it.

> Ruggiero il qual piú grazïosi carmi,
> piú dolce istoria non potrebbe udire,
> che dove alcun ricordo intervenisse
> de la sua donna, il pregò sí, che disse.
>
> [XXV, 25]

Ruggiero, who could not hear lovelier songs, sweeter story than where some recollection of his lady might intervene, pleaded with him so that he said this.

Pure and Sweet Speech

At the termination of the speech and of the episode, the narrator returns in propria persona to resume command of the plot line which, in a way, he never abandoned. His protest over an insignificant detail—upbraiding those writers (like Pulci) who made Aldigiero of Clermont the legitimate son of Girard de Roussillon —may or may not suggest Ariosto's own personal history, but in any case safeguards the narrator's omniscience in larger concerns.

He is omniscient, that is, in the world of his own creation. When sources and "external" reality enter the Ariostan world, they are refracted through the imagination that creates and dominates it, and are subject to the mixture of fact and fantasy it thrives on. At a highly dramatic moment in canto XLII (20–22), just after the epic duel on the Isle of Lipadusa, the narrator suddenly interrupts his account to forestall an objection that most readers at this point in the story would hardly think of making. He suggests that the sea captain Federigo Fulgoso (or Fregoso) might object that the rough topography of the island would not allow a battle among six knights. But, replies Ariosto to the imagined objection, Fulgoso may not know that an earthquake has changed the island during the intervening seven hundred years. After this, Ariosto apostrophizes Fulgoso out of all measure and asks that he not be quick to call him a liar. Fulgoso should hope Ariosto is no liar, since later in the canto (86–87) the poet also praises Bembo and Castiglione, in whose marginally fictional works Fulgoso appears among other elegant and articulate interlocutors. Aside from the specious justification of the would-be realist, Ariosto's defense of the "reality" of Lipadusa serves to heighten the dramatic role it has just played in his fiction. The apparition of the island is incongruous, not only through the changes that Ariosto effects on its topography, but also and above all because its splendid and somber isolation cuts it off from the pulsating rhythm which elsewhere drives paladins and ladies between conventional open fields and mysterious forests. It is the total lack of scenery that augments the pervasive atmosphere of hope and despair on the island (XLII, 15) and underlines the almost existential confrontation of the solitary knight with fate and destiny.

Thus, the tapestry to which Ariosto continually compares his poem cross-weaves threads of fact and of fantasy to create shaded areas of fictionalized reality and imagination which he attempts

[145]

to pass off as the truth. The meaning of this "truth" is inseparably tied to Ariosto's concept of his undertaking, to the evolving needs of his narrative, and to the importance of his message to his readers. Weaving metaphors permits him to impose familiar narrative patterns on the surface of his text. Actions and speech of characters and narrator alike are caught up in the parallel *laisse* constructions, where successive stanzas are connected by recurring phrases, reminiscent of the *chansons de geste*. Like a latter-day Turold describing a Roland-figure, the narrator intones:

> e questo fu d'orribil suono un corno,
> che fa fugire ognun che l'ode intorno.
> Dico che 'l corno è di sí orribil suono . . .
>
> [XV, 14–15]

And this was a horn with a horrible sound which makes everyone near it flee. I say that the horn has such a horrible sound . . .[5]

Also like Dante the pilgrim, Ariosto the master weaver appears in and is a part of the world he relates; he decides how much of that world, and in what ways, he will share with his reader. In this last way, the tapestry image justifies the arabesque manner in which he breaks off or picks up the narrative threads (II, 30; XIII, 81), justifies the variety of his grand design (XXII, 3), and enhances the value of his subject: "Et hanno i paladin sparsi tra loro, / come le gemme in un riccamo d'oro" (XXXIX, 17: "and the knights are scattered among them like jewels in a golden embroidery").

Two stanzas beyond this noble scene, however, the narrator remembers Astolfo, who has already caught up short his creator for having forgotten him. This is the other, inescapable side of the narrator's participation in the world of his creation, because the *Furioso*, like the *Roland*, is as much about human failure as achievement. His mask is never firmly in place, and his tentative use of it is characteristic of his exploratory poem. He invites his reader to pick up the loose ends of the plot, "(se 'l vi raccorda)" (XXII, 72: "[if you remember it]"), while he himself strews the landscape with fragments, strands, and remnants, and does not much seem to care. The heavily corrected manuscript of the *Furioso* affirms his many changes of mind, but belies any insouciance on his part. He knew that he would alter or eliminate whatever he had written, and therefore used only the right-hand side of the paper, leaving the other side for corrections. The narrator's lighthearted and ingenious incompetence, then, becomes a caricature of the standard picture of brooding genius. Possessing the large view of his world, he loses track of its details. A few chance examples in a single canto will suffice to make the point. As the poem moves through its shifting moods, we are told that the pagan army has been gathered so that Agramante can review his troops (XII, 72); the narrator reiterates this purpose a little later, commenting at the same time on the many strands of his huge web (XIII, 81), but he seems to get tangled in that web by making the purpose of the assembly the necessity of giving an escort to Stordilano's daughter (XIV, 40). Shortly thereafter, Mandricardo kidnaps Doralice, which the narrator relates as through a haze and "leaves to each man's judgment" (64). Wandering toward a pleasant spot, they see two knights and a lady lounging in the shade by the bank of a stream (65), leaving the narrator to discourse on his towering fantasy. Yet when in XXIII, 70, we see this action from the vantage point of the two knights (Orlando and Zerbino), they are already armed and ready for war when Mandricardo meets them. Finally, at the end of canto XIV, we witness the imponderable exploits of Rodomonte, who throws a certain Andropono from a high tower (124), and later (XVIII, 177) Andropono is killed by Medoro, leaving us to conclude either that the stout soldier-priest survived a great fall or else that Ariosto became overwhelmed by, and lost track of, his huge cast of characters.

Such confusion is not without its possible justifications. Transformation of Andropono from a priest into a gambling soldier is consistent with Ariosto's satire on clerical manners, and the evolution of warring motives into courtesy, of courtesy into a military posture in the first two cases is one further illustration of the mixture of motives expressed by the poem's opening verse. Other loose ends could be explained by appealing to the changing psychological states of the principals; when Angelica claims that she has no hope of ever returning to her father's kingdom (VIII, 4), after having insisted earlier that she is driven on by that very hope (I, 54), we may simply be observing the prime *donna mobile* in the story who, by this time, has suffered many indignities and has good reason for abandoning hope. When Orlando leaves

Zerbino and sets out after Mandricardo, but instead finds the telltale wake of Angelica and Medoro, we are told that Zerbino departed by a different road (XXIII, 99); later we learn that the two knights actually followed the same road (XXIV, 15). On a level of factual discourse, Ariosto is caught in an inconsistency. When taken as the rich and multivalent symbol it is, however, the road of the mind and the labyrinth of the heart are forever ambiguous and contradictory. In a sense, both characters are at the crossroads of their lives here in the middle of the work. Zerbino will soon die and Orlando too will soon die to his former self, only to be reborn. Both men fall in love, but the affective scenes of their passion differ as dramatic pathos differs from terror (XXIV, 5, 76).

Aside from the internal inconsistencies of the work that contribute to its satiric and psychological unity, the madness in the author's method coincides with the image of himself which he attempts to convey. Dispensing with his habitual reflective preamble, the narrator purports to launch directly into the material of canto XXXII; but instead he retraces his steps and trips over himself in the midst of admissions that he has forgotten stories he had promised to relate and that his story line seems to have gotten away fom him. Whereas Pulci came to sympathize with the matter he set out to burlesque, and Cervantes discovered deeper and broader meaning in the second part of *Don Quixote* than he had at first intended, the narrator of the *Furioso* is increasingly beset by a bad memory, factual ignorance, or simply indifference.[6] These admissions of fallibility facilitate the narrator's mediation in the lives of his characters as one of them, and at the same time emphasize the control he wields over their stories. He is so moved by Angelica's vulnerability to the Orca that he is compelled to turn to another thread in his plot (VIII, 66), and, because he must relate the betrayal of Olimpia by Bireno in canto X, he despairs that he and his reader cannot attend their wedding, which he promised at the end of canto IX. Cited a few pages back as an example of the multiple contradictions in the *Furioso*, canto XIV is also a miniature case of the way in which the progressive humanizing of the narrator is instrumental in controlling —or seeming to control—narrative point of view. The canto opens with a sweeping evaluation of the battle of Ravenna and ends with the narrator tired and out of breath. At the beginning he attempts to predispose the reader's response in a manner that is almost too blatant to be successful, unless he has already won us over and made us willing to suspend all disbelief: "Vuo' che tu tolga / di tutto il gregge pel maggior ribaldo" (24: "I want you to take him for the worst rascal in the bunch"). The reader of the Olimpia-Bireno incident is already familiar with the narrator's attempt at directing the emotions of his audience (X, 4), and he will again meet this attempt in the Zerbino-Isabella sequence (XX, 141). As he moves through canto XIV and relates the siege of Paris, however, he has difficulty keeping pace with these creatures of his imagination. Although he transcends them in his vision, he falls behind them in his action: "Deh perché a muover men son io la penna, / che quelle genti a muover l'arme pronte?" (108: "Ah! why am I less ready in moving my pen than those men in moving their arms?").

From his privileged position the narrator superintends his characters by knowing what will become of them and what forces shape their lives, and up to the end of his narrative he continues to interpret their thoughts and feelings: "par che gli dica . . . (parean con maraviglia dir tra loro) . . ." (XLVI, 89–90: "he seems to tell him . . . [marvelling, they seem to say among themselves] . . ."). He is able to translate their moods because he has created them, but also because he has a mind like theirs and is subject to the same emotions, especially love. As Orlando's madness gains momentum, the narrator gradually reveals that he too suffers from the same illness, and partially explains the alternating amusement and deep sympathy he feels for Orlando: "Credete a chi n'ha fatto esperimento" (XXIII, 112: "Believe one who has experienced it"). This is not the madness that wafts the poet above other men and opens his prophetic eye, but rather the madness of love that equates him with common humanity and blinds him to his plight. In a moment of lucidity he realizes his affinity with Orlando. Answering the objection that he sees Orlando's error and not his own, he says:

> Io vi rispondo che comprendo assai,
> or che di mente ho lucido intervallo;
> et ho gran cura (e spero farlo ormai)
> di riposarmi e d'uscir fuor di ballo:

ma tosto far, come vorrei, nol posso;
che 'l male è penetrato infin all'osso.

[XXIV, 3]

I answer you that I understand well, now that my mind has a lucid
interval; and I take great care (and hope to do so henceforth) to rest
and to leave the dance: but I cannot do it as quickly as I would like
because the illness has penetrated clear to my bones.

The porous memory, ignorance, and general fallibility that
plague him in the second half of the poem are consonant with the
differentiation he establishes between his folly and God's wisdom
and with the parallel he stresses between himself and Orlando.
Canto XXX begins with such a differentiation and parallel, which
he offers to the ladies in his audience as an explanation and
justification of his ambivalent attitude toward women.[7] We finally
glimpse the biographical Ariosto behind the mask of his fictional
narrator when he again implicitly addresses his courtly audience
(XLII, 93–95). Here he brings together the gift of prophecy that
ennobles the poem and the consuming love that enforces his
humanity; parading a gallery of statues that foretell Ferrarese
greatness, he includes a statue of his beloved Alessandra, though
he himself remains discreetly anonymous.

In becoming the beneficiary and victim of his irony, the narrator
ultimately becomes analogous, not to a pantocrator, but rather to
a creator who experiences the joys and suffering of his creatures.
Turning his irony back upon himself, the role he assigns to himself translates and magnifies the condition of those characters
who are aware of their own will and impulses yet whose destiny
detours them from the path they have chosen and leads them
astray. Since he himself is engaged in and by this world, the
attitude of the creator is not so much one of indifference as one
of fraternity and benevolence. He leaves aside speculation on the
immovable harmony beyond the moon and concentrates on that
body only insofar as it reflects on earthly concerns as a "little
earth." Acceptance of these concerns is a token of his acceptance
of humanity, and this receptivity excludes indifference and insol-
uble tragic conflict. The *Furioso* does, of course, deal largely with
conflict, frustrated love, and death, but it deprives them of their
pure factuality. The tragic mode is projected into the future, as
with the announced death of Ruggiero, but there it serves a higher

purpose and is thus justified; or else it is projected into the past where the mythical truth of the Fall from Grace is transformed into elegiac sentiment. Truth reveals its secrets only to those who search for it in the total complexity of the human microcosm where past and future, will and nature come together, where the ever-changing history of man's relationship to the mystical non-verbal world of the beast relates the tension between natural man and civilized society. In watching the knights and ladies of the *Furioso* follow the path of the mind, we learn, along with Rinaldo and others, that the road is endless, that in travelling it we will find not utopia but ourselves.

II *Immortal and Glorious*

Later generations and centuries have seen their image reflected to such a vast degree in the *Furioso* that the extent of its impact can be only suggested here. The contribution of the work can be measured as much by the distortions it underwent as by the preservation of its spirit, and the authority of the statement it makes in literary history can be appreciated by the degree both of enthusiastic adherence and rabid opposition it generated.[8] Stimulated by the Counter Reformation and the growing tendency in the second half of the sixteenth century to use Aristotle's *Poetics* as an absolute reference point for literary canons, the *Furioso* became a test case in a literary debate with theological and philosophical overtones that centered on various, frequently modulated, oppositions: of religiosity and immorality; of reverence for the ancients and the need to update; of the unified action of the epic and the multiple episodes of romance; of figurative description that could be allegorized and thus moralized, and sensual, plastic images existing on their own terms; of the poet's necessary assent to universal principles and his natural inspiration. Debates of this nature were somewhat idle in their inception because Ariosto's poem embraces all of these polarities in one degree or another and because champions of Ariosto such as Dolce, Pigna, and Giraldi Cintio exaggerated or misrepresented some of the basic tenets of their arguments, while his antagonists show the obvious superiority of the *Furioso* by the very works with which they oppose it. Trissino's *Italia liberata dei Goti* obeyed the precept that a work should be a well-unified balance, yet it had few admirers, and the *Furioso*, censured by Trissino for breaking the rule, was widely admired. Furthermore, enthusiasts of Ariosto, such as the Pléiade poets, were forced by the spare compass of their works to isolate the nobility of Zerbino's love for Isabella, the figurative liberation by Logistilla, or the sensual agony of Olimpia, and in so doing they imposed unity on the heterogeneity of the thesaurus they plundered.

Battle lines became more clearly drawn after the publication of Tasso's *Gerusalemme liberata* in 1581. Friends, relatives, or disinterested critics of both poets still based their attack and defense on the propriety of allowing Aristotle, or rather extrapolations from the *Poetics*, to dictate the nature of poetry at a remove of nearly two millennia. Proceeding from the assumption that works of different character and intent can be preferentially ranked, supporters of the *Gerusalemme* held that its better proportioned structure was a finer exemplar of heroic poetry, as were its nobler characters, and that the trajectory of Tasso's thought was more decorous and crystalline than the often rambling intricacies of Ariosto's *ottava rima*. By exaggerating Ariosto's regularities, advocates of a pure Tuscan tongue (*cruscanti*) looked to the *Furioso* as a model. It was Tasso himself, in the *Discorsi del poema eroico* of 1594, who altered his earlier stand and applauded the "errors" of the *Furioso*.

The fortunes of the poem continued to fall and rise around the turn of the sixteenth century, although the volume of editions, well over one hundred in the 1500s alone, began to tail off. Readers such as Galileo, whose outlook was formed by Renaissance institutions, continued to prefer the subtle harmonies of the work over the imputed sterility of Tasso's masterpiece. Heavy-handed academicians like Benedetto Fioretti, guided by the ideology of his time and the rhetorician's desire to categorize rules of art in his *Proginnasmi poetici*, criticized Ariosto's anachronisms and interweaving of pagan and Christian motivations among his characters, but isolated, in order to laud, the emotional realism of Isabella's lament and Orlando's madness. This adaptation of the work to polemic or political ends, the systematizing and thus the fragmenting of the total Ariostan perspective, and the corresponding preservation of its isolated glimpses into reality, was the fate of the *Furioso* throughout Europe.

While the *Furioso* retained its popularity and Ariosto's stories still had appeal, the complex vision of the mission of knighthood held the imagination less than the fascination with idealized love and a spirit purely of adventure. Montaigne, an astute critic of empty nobility, one of the least systematic of French thinkers and the one most likely to value Ariosto's "undulating and diverse" picture of man's nature, cites the superiority of Bradamante over Angelica near the end of one of his most systematic essays ("De l'institution des enfants") as a type of "manly but not mannish" virtue that should be emulated. And imitated it was in plays like the *Bradamante* of Robert Garnier and later of Thomas Corneille. Although the *Furioso* sustained a wide readership, for La Fontaine and others the intricate strands of Ariosto's tapestry were susceptible to unraveling and retelling in the form of short stories or mere tales of adventure. In Golden Age Spain the survival of Carolingian themes in the sixteenth century was helped along by compendia (*Cancionero de romances, Silva de varios romances,* and the like) in which chivalric and *morisco* legends, historical chronicles, and pastoral fancies stand side by side. But instead of producing a cross-weaving of genre and style, restatement of Ariostan motifs led to the dissolution of love and arms and to the opposition and usual preference of the former to the latter. Opposition is at times so pronounced and apparently conscious that Alonso de Ercilla's *La Araucana* begins on the pointedly contrastive note "No las damas, amor, no gentilezas . . ."

The year 1602 is a convenient one for seeing the way in which the *Furioso* came to mean all things to all minds. In that year Lope de Vega's poem "La hermosura de Angélica" delights in the many adventures, digressions, and reversals that befall those who profess arms and confess love, but, also in the same year, Góngora's pastoral poetry takes the episode of Angelica and Medoro as an ideal and impossible moment of love frozen in time. It was Cervantes in the *Galatea* and *Quixote* who came the closest to the pose of the Ariostan narrator who views his work as a complex web and, standing both in and apart from his story, ironically alleges that he is subject to the whims of his work. But even in the long digression called "El curioso impertinente," which faithfully elaborates the action of canto LXIII dealing with conjugal faithfulness and infidelity, Cervantes' interjection that the tale "contains enclosed moral secrets worthy of being heeded, heard, and imitated" is programmatic where Ariosto is illusive and suggestive.

Relegation of the *Furioso* to a series of adventure stories or the willingness to moralize its episodes and read them as an allegorical complex à la Fornari and Toscanella may not entirely explain the vogue of the poem in Elizabethan England, but they did become its common lot. Putting aside the problematic question of Continental influence on Wyatt and Surrey, the first trickle of Ariosto's fame took shape in Peter Beverley's version of the *Tragicall and Pleasant Historie of Ariodanto and Ienevra* (1565); Mario Praz is probably correct in suggesting that the Scottish local color in the story explains part of its success. Both allegorical complexity and adaptation of the *Furioso* to a foreign political scene culminate in the *Faerie Queene*, the supreme instance of Ariosto's impact on European literature. It has been frequently claimed, almost truistically, that without the example of the *Furioso* Spenser's poem would not exist in its present form. Spenser's adaptation of plot and character and the debt of the Spenserian stanza to the *ottava rima* are all well documented. But the inflections in Ariosto's poetic voice are too idiosyncratic and Spenser's imagination is too powerful and unswervingly directed for us to speak of anything but widely divergent variations on basic chivalric themes. Guyon, the Hero of Temperance, is endowed from the outset by his creator with the exemplary virtue that rarely fails him of seeing through "guileful semblants," and his destruction of Acrasia's Bower of Bliss is inevitable; but his approximate counterpart, Ruggiero, who is equally predestined, is seen as Alcina's victim and is always shown in the agonizing process of becoming worthy. If Florimell and False (or "Snowy") Florimell came from Angelica, then we are witness to the separation of chiaroscuro into the radiance of chastity and the shadow of vice. Did Spenser really move radically in the direction of Ariostan romance in the last few books? [9] The heavily allegorized love of the highborn Aemylia for the lowly Amyas in Book IV argues against such a dramatic change and lacks the enigmatic flavor of the love of Angelica and Medoro that has perplexed centuries of commentators. After Spenser, and with the possible exception of *Much Ado About Nothing* and *A Midsummer Night's Dream*, the history of Ariosto in England is more a matter of presence than genuine influence.

Although critics continued to drag out the Ariosto-Tasso controversy, at the end of the seventeenth century and the beginning of the eighteenth the desire to dissect the poem and rearrange it along the lines of Cartesian reason gave way to the realization that the heart has its reasons which Reason may not know. Vincenzo Gravina's *Della ragion poetica* (1708) marks a new open-mindedness toward the irregularities of the *Furioso* and toward the coexistence of the marvelous and the real. Near the end of his life Alfieri favorably revalued his concept of the poem and reaffirmed the need to approach it as an organic whole. Guided by the fustian reasoning of Giuseppe Baretti and even more by the good sense of Saverio Bettineli, Voltaire also revised his estimation of Ariosto. It remained only for Goethe's high, if purple, praise to cap the gradual revival of the *Furioso* in the eighteenth century.

Following Bettinelli, and more than Manzoni and Leopardi after him, the first modern reader of Ariosto is Foscolo. The confluence of classic form at odds with romantic inspiration in his own work and the combined aspiration and disappointment in his life gave Foscolo a deep appreciation of Ariosto's many ironies. He understood that Renaissance imitation and modern concepts of inspiration are not antithetical, and he was aware that after the first few readings the confusing and cluttered world of the *Furioso* gives rise to an endless sense of harmonies which vary with each subsequent reading. This is close to the experience of most readers of Ariosto, and the lesson could have been better learned by the wave of idealist philosophers that was yet to come. For Hegel, the attitude of the *Furioso* toward medieval chivalry and the author's ironies could best be explained as a sociological phenomenon and a crisis of historical conscience. Application of Hegelian dialectic to literature shaped Ariosto criticism of following generations. Out of the clash of antithetical forces, of the Renaissance confronting the Middle Ages, came a synthesis which for Vincenzo Gioberti was a tension between the real and the ideal, for De Sanctis was pure art, and for Croce was ideal harmony. As brilliant as some of the pages undoubtedly are in De Sanctis' Zurich lectures (1858–59) and the *Storia della letteratura italiana* (1872), he and especially Croce tend excessively to systematize the poem's eternal ebb and flow and to abstract the poet from a world in which he is ultimately engaged.

In more recent years, this idealism has been tested and tempered by close textual analysis. As a result, Carducci's *Saggio su* l' "*Orlando Furioso,*" and after him Gianfranco Contini's *Come lavorava l'Ariosto,* the auroral studies of Debenedetti, Binni, Lanfranco Caretti, and Cesare Segre have all examined stylistic corrections and given a textual basis to Ariosto's artistic consciousness; on the other hand, Giovanni Cesareo's *La Fantasia dell'Ariosto* has put Rajna's positivistic source hunting into perspective and restored the imaginative refraction of Ariosto's borrowings. Momigliano's expert *Saggio* and Natalino Sapegno's percipient comments in his *Compendio di storia della letteratura italiana* have continued the unremitting movement away from Crocean absolutism, shading extreme positions and thus ensuring the integrity of the poem. Ventures into Freudian and general psychoanalytic criticism have shown a commendable circumspection that dogmatic Hegelianism lacks.[10] Down through the academic opposition of Ariosto and Tasso and the dialectical polarities of the real and the ideal, the permanence of the *Furioso* has been its ability to galvanize critical discussions and reflect the changing moods of different generations. Reading the work through the eyes of Aristotle or Descartes, Hegel or Freud, may seem to violate its fragile ironies and its commitment to the moment and milieu of Renaissance Ferrara. But if an alert reading of the *Orlando Furioso* teaches us anything, it is that reality has many facets and truth lies in the mind of the beholder.

Notes and References

Preface

1. The 3,624 entries made by Giuseppe Fatini are an adequate measure of the volume of studies written on Ariosto and his works, in *Bibliografia della critica ariostea, 1510–1956* (Florence: Le Monnier, 1958).

Chapter One

1. *Maranos* in fact sought refuge in Ferrara from the Spaniards until the wave of heretic persecutions at the end of the fifteenth century. In his *Negromante* Ariosto describes his protagonist as "a Jew by origin, one of those that were chased from Castile" (I, i). Cf. the satire to Bembo, vv. 34–36.

2. See C. A. Patrides, " 'The Bloody and Cruell Turke': The Background of a Renaissance Commonplace," *Studies in the Renaissance,* 10 (1963), 126–35, esp. 130–31.

3. References to these and other weighty events enter the fabric of most of Ariosto's works merely as casual allusions to current happenings. Cf. *Il Negromante*, V, iii.

4. See the *Diario Ferrarese* in Lodovico Muratori's *Scriptores rerum Ithalicarum* (Milan: Societas palatina, 1723–51), 24, col. 347.

5. The apparent original source of the story is Giovan Battista Pigna, *La vita di M. Lodovico Ariosto* in *I Romanzi* (Venice: Valgrisi, 1554).

6. Michele Catalano, Ariosto's principal biographer, gives a full description of the drab routine that must have been Ariosto's life in the service of Cardinal Ippolito, in *Vita di Ludovico Ariosto* (Geneva: Olschki, 1930–31), vol. 1, pp. 204–205.

7. Ariosto's various letters from Garfagnana give clear evidence of his administrative conscientiousness, compassion for his constituents, and shrewdness in handling their affairs, and of the limitations on his effectiveness imposed by ducal politics. *Lettere*, edited by Angelo Stella (Milan: Mondadori, 1965).

Chapter Two

1. See *Diario Ferrarese*, 24, Col. 404; and Julia Cartwright, *Baldassare Castiglione, His Life and Letters* (London: J. Murray, 1908), vol. 1, pp. 338–42.

2. As Trissino insisted in *Poetica* (1529), VI. In 1554 Pigna judged *La Cassaria* to be better than *I Suppositi* on the basis of plot construction (see Bernard Weinberg's discussion in *A History of Literary Criticism in the Italian Renaissance* [Chicago: University of Chicago Press, 1961], vol. 1, p. 451). The second prologue to *I Suppositi* diverges from the impersonal verve of New Comedy by implicitly censuring the moral license of Aretino's comedies.

3. Francesco De Sanctis, *Opere*, edited by Niccolò Gallo (Milan and Naples: Ricciardi, 1961), p. 430.

4. Critics commonly cite the letter written by Alfonso Paolucci to Alfonso I, describing the regal splendor of the setting and the pageantry hosted by the Pope himself, and other letters describing the scene that depicted Ferrara "precisely as it is." See Edmund Gardner, *The King of Court Poets: A Study of the Work, Life and Times of Ludovico Ariosto* (London: Constable, 1906), pp. 329–31; Aldo Borlenghi, ed., *Commedie del Cinquecento* (Milan: Rizzoli, 1959), vol. 1, p. 986.

5. The use of such contemporary allusions to lend greater credence to discoveries was discussed by theoreticians like G. B. Giraldi Cintio (*Scritti estetici di G. B. Giraldi Cintio*, edited by G. Antimaco [Milan: Daelli, 1864], vol. 1, pp. 62–68) and criticized—even while they used it—by playwrights like Lasca (see *La Gelosia*, preface). Cf. Rabelais, II, 9.

6. Guido Marpillero long ago made the persuasive case that Ariosto also had the *Decameron* (VII, 7) in mind. "I Suppositi di Lodovico Ariosto," *Giornale storica della letteratura italiana,* 21 (1898), pp. 299–301.

7. Giraldi Cintio remains somewhat equivocal and argues against the use of *rhymed* verse for comedy; while censuring the *sdrucciolo*, he applauds Arisoto as the peerless writer of comedy in this age.

8. *Lettere*, no. 202, p. 366, April 5, 1532.

9. This is perhaps what Giacomo Grillo had in mind when he refers to Ariosto's play *Cassandra*, confusing the *Cassaria* with the *Calandria* (*Poets at the Court of Ferrara, Ariosto, Tasso and Guarini* [Boston: Excelsior Press, 1943], p. 19). Grillo's unacknowledged verbatim borrowings (p. 12; Gardner, pp. 2, 7) are indicative of the extent to which Gardner's influence in this country has never been adequately recognized.

10. *De hominis dignitate*, edited by Eugenio Garin (Florence: Vallecchi, 1942), pp. 149–54. A young man from Ferrara, claiming to possess the secrets of necromancy, exorcism, and alchemy, completely beguiled Lodovico Sforza, to the complete disgust of Leonardo; see *I manoscritti: dell'anatomia*, edited by Theodor Sabachnikoff (Paris: Rouveyre, 1898), II, 242vo (N).

Notes and References

11. For a substantially different opinion on this matter, see Walter Binni, *Ludovico Ariosto,* Turin: Eri, 1968), p. 37.

12. Aristotle, *Ethics,* IV, 8, 1127a ff.; Horace, *Saturae* I, iv, 35, 85.

13. "Cotidianae vitae speculum," cf. Horace, *Sat.* II, 10.

14. Horace, *Odes,* II, iii, 25–26. The closing lines of this diptych come from Catullus.

15. The most authoritative manuscript we possess is the one in the Municipal Library in Ferrara. It is marked by authorial corrections and marginalia that evince a Horatian "limae labor" and recall the manuscript of the *Furioso.* Although it is unsigned, the unfulfilled promise on the title page to furnish two additional satires in no may invalidates the authenticity of the manuscript; rather, it may express the author's unfulfilled intention.

16. *Sat.* I, iv, 33.

17. Cf. *Lettere,* no. 14, p. 28. The eyeglass mentioned in the letter recalls the portrait of Leo X in the Uffizi Gallery done by Raphael where it appears as a magnifying glass for studying miniature illuminations in prayer books. Ariosto, however, implies that the pontiff had dim vision, especially when it came to noticing the corruption that surrounded him.

18. Walter Binni claims February, 1523, as the correct date for this piece, Catalano dates it in the summer of 1521, but Cesare Segre (*Opere minori* [Milan and Naples: Ricciardi, 1954]) cites biographical documents on Lucrezia Pio, whose death in 1520 would place the satire in 1519.

19. The word "cavallar" falls far short of the dignity 'cavaliere" would have had.

20. *Lettere,* no. 190, p. 347.

21. *Ars poetica,* 89, 240ff; *Sat.* iv, 9, and vi, 17; *Epistulae* II, i, 168–69, 250–51.

22. See Giuseppe Fatini, "Su la fortuna e l'autenticità delle liriche di Ludovico Arosto," *Giornale storico della letteratura italiana,* sup. 22–23, 1924.

23. XXXVI, on the election of Julius II; XXXVII, on the death of Pandolfo; XXXVIII, on a Ferrarese victory over Spain; XXXIX, a diatribe against Alfonso Trotto; XL, the routine praise of Vittoria Colonna.

24. Cf. the *Capitolo* (XXVII) that rings in lines from Petrarch as refrains after every third verse.

25. The first poem that we have of Ariosto, lamenting the death of Eleanor of Aragon (Oct. 11, 1493), draws on Petrarch's *Triumph of Death,* the sourcebook of hundreds of mortuary elegies in the fifteenth and sixteenth centuries.

26. Tebaldeo, "Io son quel che io fui"; Boiardo, *Armorum libri,* I.

57; Petrarch, *Rime* CXLV. Cf. the *contaminatio* of Ariosto and Petrarch in Du Bellay's *Olive* XCIII.

27. "On all sides the wind and ocean beat . . . [never] have I changed place, nor will I ever change"; ". . . than the vain wind, vain the ebb flux . . ." Cf. Horace, *Epist.* I, viii, 12; *Ap.*, 268–69; *Sat.* II, vi, 80–81; Ovid, *Amores* III, iv, 40, ix, i; *OF*, XXIX, 29, v. 8.

28. See Alfonso Sammut, *La Fortuna dell'Ariosto nell'Inghilterra elisabettiana* (Milan: Vita e Pensiero, 1971), p. 79.

29. Alexandre Cioranescu, *L'Arioste en France des origines à la fin du XVIIIᵉ siècle* (Paris: Les Editions des Presses Modernes, 1939), vol. 1, pp. 295–99.

30. Cf. Dámaso Alonso, "Un soneto de Francisco Medrano imitado de Ariosto," *Hispanic Review*, 16 (1948), 162–64.

31. See Joseph Vianey, "L'Arioste et la Pléiade," *Bulletin italien*, 1 (1901), 295–317, and Alice Cameron, *The Influence of Ariosto's Epic and Lyric Poetry on Ronsard and his Group* (Baltimore: Johns Hopkins Press, 1930).

32. *Comedie très elegante, en laquelle sont contenues les amours récréatives d'Erostrate, fils de Philogone de Catania. . . .*

33. See Felix Schelling, *The Life and Writings of George Gascoigne* (New York: Russell and Russell, 1967), p. 44.

Chapter Three

1. *The Allegory of Love* (London, Oxford and New York: Oxford University Press, 1971), p. 309.

2. His concept of love is not as spiritual as that of Chaucer's Prioress who wore the same motto on her brooch, and yet is more serious than Leonardo's "amor onni cose vince" which gave itself to playful word games, "Vittoria vince e vinci tu vittore."

3. See G. B. Giraldi Cintio, *Discorsi intorno al comporre dei romanzi* in *Scritti estetici*, vol. 1, p. 140.

4. *Aeneid*, I, i, and *Purgatorio*, XIV, 109–10; *Aeneid*, XII, 950–53, and *Inferno*, VIII, 46.

5. ". . . now that I have come out of the caves and lairs of wild animals and returned to the company of men. I cannot yet speak of our dangers: 'the mind is horrified of memories and seeks refuge from pain,' and on the other hand . . ." *Lettere*, no. 13, p. 26, October 1, 1512. Cf. *Inferno*, I, 6.

6. Allan Gilbert, "The Sea-Monster in Ariosto's *Cinque Canti* and in *Pinocchio*," *Italica*, 33 (1956), 260–64.

7. Donald Carne-Ross has luminously suggested that a double reference to the *Aeneid* in canto VIII, the one in which Orlando appears for the first time, lends him something of Dido's passion and something

of Aeneas' sense of duty. "The One and the Many," *Arion*, 5 (1966), 224. This duality will be explored in a later chapter.

8. Distortion of the idea led to Machiavelli's reputation in France as a scoundrel. See Innocent Gentillet, *Discours sur les moyens de bien gouverner et maintenir en bonne paix un royaume ou autre principauté . . . contre Nicholas Machiavel* (n.p., 1579), p. 429. The 1576 edition has been reprinted by C. Edward Rathé (Geneva: Droz, 1968). Dealing with the idea of political deceit, Montaigne closes the numerically central chapter of *Essais* II with "not having been able to do what they wished, they pretended to wish for what they were able to do," and begins the middle essay of the third book with the same idea. Cf. Petrarch, *Rime* CXVIII.

9. After having been quoted by Publius Syrus and Laberius, commented on at length by Seneca in *De ira*, I, xx, 4–5, and paraphrased by Macrobius, *Saturnalia*, II, vii, 20: "necesse est multos timeat quem timent multi." George Puttenham cites an anonymous poet of the time, "Much must he be beloved, that loveth much, / Feare many must he needs, whom many fear," *The Arte of English Poesie* (1559), edited by Alice Walker and Gladys Willcock (Cambridge: Cambridge University Press, 1939), p. 200.

10. Croce speaks of Ariosto's contempt for the judges, soldiers, politicians, and clerics of his age, but "ends by accepting his own times and respecting the powerful personages who have finally prevailed," *Ariosto, Shakespeare e Corneille* (Bari: Laterza, 1961), p. 38. I prefer to stress the shifting tension between the extremes of aspiration and resignation.

11. It did occur to Agrippa von Nettesheim in 1531 to object to flatterers who deduced the pedigree of their princes by aligning them with Arthur and Tristam; this, in his view, was "worse than the mad dreams of poets," *De incertitudine et vanitate scientiarum at artium*, V.

12. At the risk of quoting them out of context, two astute readers of Ariosto have claimed that he "was serious about the d'Estes" (Thomas Greene, *The Descent from Heaven, A Study in Epic Continuity* [New Haven: Yale University Press, 1963], p. 133), yet paid them "a *seemingly* handsome compliment" (emphasis added: A. Bartlett Giamatti, *The Earthly Paradise and the Renaissance Epic* [Princeton: Princeton University Press, 1966], p. 152). Both writers are correct, for reasons I hope to make obvious. Augusto Turati views the heroes of the poem as type projections of the vices and virtues inherent in Renaissance courtly manners. "Ruggiero e Bradamante," in *L'Ottava d'oro* (Milan and Verona: Mondadori, 1933), pp. 413–36.

13. Like the final edition of Montaigne's *Essais*, Ariosto's third edition increased the number of chapters and considerably retouched episodes he had written years before, even to the extent of transposing

events. Cf. Allan Gilbert, *Orlando Furioso* (New York: Vanni, 1954), vol. 1, p. xxi, and Santorre Debenedetti, *I frammenti autografi dell' Orlando Furioso* (Turin: Chiantore, 1937).

14. The observation is made by Carne-Ross, "The One and the Many," pp. 223, 229.

15. Cf. *La Chanson de Roland*, vv. 1198–1204, and Rabelais, I, 44.

16. Cf. Bembo, *Prose scelte* (Milan: Sonzogno, 1880), p. 42.

17. Grifone need not have worried, however, because, according to Honoré Bonet's *L'Arbre des batailles* (1387), "Those who wear the arms of another in order to commit a fraud must be punished" (IV, cxviii).

18. Moreover, without a trace of irony, Ariosto's *Capitoli* XV sets off the vulgar rabble from the knight's faithfulness to his sacrosanct pledge: "Per la vil plebe è fatto il giuramento; / Ma tra gli spirti più elevati sono / Le semplici promesse un sagramento" (vv. 46–48: "The common herd takes an oath; but among more elevated spirits simple promises are a sacrament") Cf. *OF*, XXI, 68.

19. Cf. the story of courtly *noblesse oblige* reported by Pierre Belperron in *La Joie d'amour* (Paris: Plon, 1948), pp. 22–23.

20. "Cerca far *morir* lei, che morir *merta*, / e serva a più tuo *onor* tu la tua *morte*." (V, 54, ff.; emphasis added: "Try to make her die who deserves to die, and your own death for your greater honor.")

21. Cf. Ariosto's comment on seeking fame: "né gli [man] convenga andare a piè, se astretto è di mutar paese" (*Sat.* III, 250–51): "nor does it suit him to go on foot if he is forced to change regions"). Justius Lipsius, *De constantia*, I, iii.

22. Cf. XXIV, 105.

23. With both levity and seriousness, the *Satire* stress the similarity of creatures. In the second he speaks of his lodging that accommodated four animals: a mule, an old horse, his servant, and himself, vv. 13–15. See also VI, 100–02; VII, 64ff.

24. For Ariosto's attitude toward ancient and modern warfare and toward the stages of composition in the *Furioso* as they were affected by changes in political alliance, see Robert Durling, *The Figure of the Poet in Renaissance Epic* (Cambridge, Mass.: Harvard University Press, 1965), pp. 139–42; Vincenzo Gioberti, *Primato morale e civile degli italiani* in *Opere* (Milan: Bocca, 1939), II, 153. Guicciardini describes the French expedition into Italy as the invasion of an Arcadian paradise which is shocked into reality by the roar of thirty-six brass cannons, this German invention "più tosto diabolico che umano instrumento." Still, the French forces lack "la medesima virtú," *Storia d'Italia* (Bari: Laterza, 1967), pp. 2, 63–68, 71–74. See also Julius Molinaro, "Ariosto and the Seven Deadly Sins," *Forum Italicum*, 3 (June, 1969), 253–54.

Notes and References

25. E.g., XLV, 75. On the Renaissance "fianchi," Ariosto builds medieval "alte torri," all within the scope of a recollection of *Aeneid* V, 439–42, where Vergil decribes the collossal battle of Dares and Entellus. John Arthos mentions that Christian paracletic intervention is consonant with the Crusade atmosphere, where interference by classical gods would not have been, but beyond that also pertains to the Dukes of Ferrara in the story and in Ariosto's readership. *On the Poetry of Spenser and the Form of Romances* (London: George Allen and Unwin, 1956), p. 125.

26. For Alfonso as a *cavalliero erante*, see Bartolommeo Fontana, *Renata di Francia* (Rome: Forzani, 1889), 1, 155.

27. Cf. Montaigne: "The stars have fatally destined the state of Rome for an example of what they could do in this kind; in it are comprised all the forms and adventures that concern a state: all that order or disorder, good or evil fortune, can do." *Essais*, III, 9, and Torquato Tasso, *Poema eroico* in *Prose*, edited by Francesco Flora (Milan and Rome: Rizzoli, 1935), pp. 411–12.

Chapter Four

1. For an excellent summation of this debate, see Bernard Weinberg, *A History of Literary Criticism in the Italian Renaissance*, vol. 2, pp. 954–1073.

2. *Lettere*, no. 16, p. 31, Oct. 25, 1515.

3. An examination of this situation from the point of view of authorial participation and intervention is found in Durling, *The Figure of the Poet in Renaissance Epic*, pp. 150–60. For a convenient but perhaps misleading typology of Ariostan womanhood, see Fausto Bianchi, "Eterno femminino ariosteo," *L'Ottava d'oro*, pp. 313–36.

4. "Significa la forza delle virtuose operationi, che fanno altrui cadere, e levare de suoi mali habiti," *Orlando Furioso* (Venice: Valvassori, 1553), VI. A commendably thorough account of the allegorized commentaries on the shield is found in Paul Alpers, *The Poetry of the Faerie Queene* (Princeton: Princeton University Press, 1967), pp. 160–74.

5. Jacopo Sannazaro, *Opere volgari* (Bari: Laterza, 1961), pp. 156, 188, 227, 247. In this last instance Sannazaro does conclude that, despite the testimony of the Roman ruins, only the person who follows the road to fame and glory is really happy.

6. Pio Raja (*Le fonti dell' "Orlando Furioso,"* [Florence: Sansoni, 1876], p. 475) claims the episode is of Ariosto's invention, but cf. *Il Principe*, ch. 25, and L. B. Alberti, "Cena familiaris" in *Opere volgari*, edited by Cecil Grayson (Bari: Laterza, 1960), pp. 345–56. See also the excursus on "Poetry as Perpetuation" discussed by Ernst Robert

Curtius, *European Literature and the Latin Middle Ages* (New York and Evanston: Harper and Row, 1963), pp. 476–77.

7. On this point, see Sister Joan Lechner, *Renaissance Concepts of the Commonplaces* (New York: Pageant Press, 1962), pp. 136 and 232, and Erwin Panofsky, "Metropolitan Symposium," *Renaissance News,* 5 (1952), 5–7.

8. Carne-Ross comments on Ariosto's syntactic mastery, which here embroils the individual action with the universal penchant it illustrates, in "la piena d'error casa d'Atlante" which he calls "a punning line that rhetorically enacts the confusion it describes." "The One and the Many," p. 200.

9. See Erwin Panofsky, *Hercules am Scheidewege* (Leipzig and Berlin: Teubner, 1930), and *Satire* V, 151–53, 160–68.

10. Cf. III, 63; X, 15; XXIV; 30, 89; *Il Negromante,* II, i.

11. See *Lettere,* no. 12, p. 25, July 14, 1512.

12. Cf. XXII, 46–47, XXXVII, 42, 47.

13. *Codex Atlanticus,* 39 ᵛ·. Cf. *L'Arbre des batailles,* "whether a soldier who goes out of his mind should be imprisoned" (IV, xci); the answer: no.

14. A circular letter of the Paris School of Theology in 1444 speaks of "folly, which is our second nature and seems to be inherent in man," quoted by Mikhail Bakhtin, *Rabelais and his World* (Cambridge, Mass. and London: M.I.T. Press, 1968), p. 75. Although Bakhtin scarcely mentions Ariosto, he makes many illuminating remarks on laughter and madness as they relate to saturnalia.

15. Cf. "For that which I do I allow not; for what I would, that do I not; but what I hate, that do I," Romans 7:15 (KJV); Erasmus, *Opera omnia* (Leyden, 1703–06, Gregg Press Reprint, London, 1962), vol. 7, cols. 799e–800a; Calvin, *Institution chrestienne,* II, ii, 27. For the romance antecedents to this war of opposites in Orlando and for the realistic progression of his madness, see: A. Galetti, "L'*Orlando Furioso* e l'epica medioevale," and Gaetano Boschi, "Diagnostica della pazzia di Orlando," in *L'Ottava d'oro,* pp. 103–30, 185–201.

16. See XXI, 53, and Machiavelli, *Discorsi,* III, 19–20.

17. XIV, 133; XIX, 101; XXXI, 25, 79, 84; XLV, 80.

18. Cf. Leonardo, MS. in the library of Lord Leicester in Norfolk, edited by Girolamo Calvi (Milan: Cogliati, 1909), 1ᵛ· and 36ᵛ·; MS. Arundel 263 in the British Museum, published by Danesi (Rome, 1923–30), 104ᵛ·.

19. Ariosto needed no Freud to explicate the pathetic fallacy or the projection of fear or desire in dreams; the observation had been made by every major preceptor of love since Ovid, e.g., *Ex ponto,* I, ii.

20. See also XVIII, 156; XXIII, 132; XXIX, 44; XXXI, 38, 45; XLIV, 2; *Satire* III, 259–67; the veil worn by Una to suggest that truth

is not always plain to see (*Faerie Queene*, I, i); and Justus Lipsius on the search for self in the castle of the mind, *De constantia*, I, ii. Reference to the four cardinal virtues in X, 59, and the implicit identification of Alcina with art, Logistilla with reason, situate the advent of Ruggiero's self-knowledge within the Thomistic opposition of art and prudence. For Aquinas, prudence is synonymous with practical reason and "comes into the soul by means of a quieting of sensory passions." *Summa Theologica*, I–II, 57, 4c; *Exposition of Aristotle's Physics*, VII, Lect. 6.

Chapter Five

1. Rajna cites other analogues of a more strictly literary nature, but which compose only a part of the Journey to Paradise lore, in *Le fonti dell' "Orlando Furioso,"* pp. 461–75; and he could have cited contemporary pastiches, like Rabelais, II, 34 (1532), of the voyage from Senapo-Prester John to the regions of the moon. Beyond the chivalric love of adventure, connected with the Romance of Alexander, such stories sprang from a spirit of exploration like the *Pantheon* of Godfrey of Viterbo, from a spirit of devotion and asceticism, and from legendary themes like the story of Seth. Trained among the Brethren of the Common Life, Erasmus saw the story of Seth as an analogue of man's ability to imitate Christ, but converted the Promethean story into a *jeu d'esprit*, in *Opus epistolarum*, edited by P. S. Allen (Oxford: Clarenon Press, 1906), vol. 1, pp. 268–71.

2. This is the orthodox medieval view found in Peter Abelard's commentary on the Works of the Six Days, in the *De situ terrarum* and *De imagine mundi*, and copied word for word by Gervase of Tilbury who, like Peter Lombard, adds that it was situated on a height touching the circle of the moon's orbit (cf. *OF*, XXXIV, 48). Saint Augustine went so far as to state that Paradise had no real existence at all but was merely an allegorical conception (*De Genesi ad litteram*, VII, i, in Migne, *Patrologia latina*, 34, cols. 371–73).

3. *Satire* III, 55–66. One of Leonardo's most advanced sketches of a flying machine is superimposed on a map of Europe that shows national and political demarcations.

4. Nearly all the maps of the late Middle Ages carried the extremities of Ethiopia far to the East and minimized the size of the Red Sea and Indian Ocean in such a way as to bring central Africa within no great distance of India. On the Jerome map of Palestine two tracts called "India Egyptii" and "India Ethiopie" were placed along the shores of the Red Sea opposite the mouths of the Indus and show such marvels as wild beasts and bearded women. Some of this confusion persisted until da Gama reached India (1498).

5. The Romans had discovered the Canary and Madeira groups and,

owing to the mild climate and favorable conditions, had associated them with the "Islands of the Blest" of Greek mythology and thus had come to call them the "Fortunate Isles." With the crystallization of Latin literary forms there appeared a stereotyped conception of ideal landscape, the *locus amoenus*, in which the essential elements were always the same: a rich meadow shaded by laurels and myrtles, and and watered by a murmuring stream (cf. *OF*, VI, 23); a placid spot where eternal spring prevails and where frost and heat are unknown (*OF*, III, 51). This formula was used by the Latin poets in describing the blessed Isles of the Hesperides and the Elysian Fields. In the Middle Ages these isles passed again into the realm of the unknown, though their traditional description was employed in picturing the Terrestrial Paradise and their memory lingered on to adorn the Western Ocean on the Beatus maps, together with more fabulous isles, and to serve as the datum point for the Western prime meridian by which mathematicians long after Ptolemy took the longitude of the earth. (See Isidore, *Etymologiae*, XIII–XIV; *De imagine mundi*, I, 10–11).

6. *Disputed Questions on Evil*, II, 6. Cf. Rabelais, III, 1.

7. Which accounted for at least forty-seven. See Josias Simler, *Commentarius de Alpibus* (Zurich: Froschoverus, 1576).

8. The language in these episodes and the attitudes they outline gain greater perspective when seen against the parable of *Satire* III, 208–31, where the inhabitants of some antediluvian period climbed to the peak of a mountain to watch the moon wax and wane, and "girar il cielo." They attempted to pillage it, but fell vainly to earth. This mountain, we are told, is the wheel of Fortune.

9. Cf. Franco Pool, *Interpretazione dell'Orlando Furioso* (Florence: La Nuova Italia, 1968), p. 235, and Erwin Panofsky, *Renaissance and Renascences* (New York: Harper and Row, 1972), pp. 92, 96, 187.

10. Donato Internoscia, "Are There Two Melissas in the *Orlando Furioso?*," *Italica*, 25 (1948), 217–26.

Chapter Six

1. De Sanctis, *Storia della letteratura italiana* (Turin: Einaudi, 1966), II, 531, 537.

2. Rudolf Gottfried, ed., *Orlando Furioso*, translated by John Harington (Bloomington and London: Indiana University Press, 1966), p. 16; Momigliano, *Saggio su l' "Orlando Furioso"* (Bari: Laterza, 1959).

3. At the beginning of the *Encomium Moriae* Erasmus claims to "have praised folly and not altogether foolishly," and concludes that "even a fool often speaks opportunely."

4. Rosemond Tuve, *Elizabethan and Metaphysical Imagery* (Chicago and London: University of Chicago Press, 1965), p. 185.

5. In the seventh satire Ariosto derided the humanistic affectation of deriving high-sounding classical names from common names through correct or false etymologies (vv. 58–63).

6. *Mutabil Fortuna,* as she is called by Fulcio in *La Cassaria* (IV, viii).

7. Cf. Rabelais, I, 27.

8. Cf. XII, 86; XXIV, 93; XLII, 58, 60; XLV, 91.

9. Ariosto frequently creates such tensions in a single canto by swaying an initially impassive nature in favor of certain momentarily favored characters and against others; cf. XXIII, 1, 8, 52, 106. Therefore, it is difficult to accept the argument of Berto Bertù that Ariosto's nautical descriptions evince a photographic interest in nature and a likely familiarity with sailing. "Il mare nell'*Orlando Furioso,*" *L'Ottava d'oro,* pp. 521–43.

10. On the other hand, Astolfo's straight-faced survey of Assyrian and Persian crowns, reduced to empty bladders (XXXIV, 76), recalls the farces played before the Este court in which clowns flayed one another with bloated pigs' bladders.

11. E.g., XII, 77; and XIV, 120; cf. *Il Negromante,* II, ii.

12. Cf. also Vergil, "Hyperboreo septem(−) subiecta trioni" ("lying under the seven northern stars of Ursa Major"), *Georgics* III, 381; *Cinque Canti,* II, 43; and *Capitoli* IV, 54. Stylistic comparisons are endless between the *Furioso* and other Renaissance works that dwell on the theme of "the lowest heaven which always gains from our loss"; cf. "che Creso o Crasso insieme non ridusse" (*OF,* XXXVIII, 2) and "Si mihi nascenti melior fortuna dedisset / Vel Croesus vel quas Crassus habebat opes," *Oeuvres poétiques de Joachim du Bellay,* edited by Henri Chamard (Paris: Droz, 1931), VI, 96. The syntax of the first two verses of the poem is analyzed by B. Terracini, "Lingua libera e libertà linguistica," *Archivo glottologico italiano,* 35 (1950), pp. 109–110.

13. *Il Cinquecento* (Milan: Vallardi, 1965), p. 189. Standard reference works for the Middle Ages have been Vincent Hopper, *Medieval Number Symbolism* (New York: Columbia University Press, 1938); the excursuses of Curtius on "numerical composition" and "numerical apothegms"; and now for the Renaissance, Christopher Butler, *Number Symbolism* (New York: Barnes and Noble, 1970). See also Charles S. Singleton, "The Poet's Number at the Center," *MLN,* 80 (January, 1965), pp. 1–10.

14. Many parallels, but by no means necessarily sources, could be cited to complement the scene, such as the seven bathings in the Jordan prescribed by Elisha to cure a Syrian general of leprosy (II Kings, 5:10). The point is that the ritual bathing in Ariosto has deep roots in biblical and magical lore.

15. Cf. XXIII, 62; XXXVI, 39; XLIII, 177; Judges 7:7. Naborre Campanini says that numerical approximations were frequent in Reggian dialect. *Ludovico Ariosto nei prologhi delle sue commedie* (Bologna: Zanichelli, 1891), p. 181. Cf. the satire to Pistofilo, v. 30.

16. See Giuseppe Ravegnani, "Vita, morte e miracoli di Rodomonte," and Giuseppe Lipparini, "Angelica e Medoro," *L'Ottava d'oro*, pp. 205–223, 393–409.

17. See Paolo Arcari, "Medoro," *L'Ottava d'oro*, pp. 227–257.

Chapter Seven

1. See Carne-Ross, "The One and the Many," p. 225, and, for other comments on the deification of the artist, Robert Durling, "The Divine Analogy in Ariosto," *MLN*, 78 (January, 1963), pp. 1–14.

2. By the "ragioni efficaci" of the hermit and the "efficaci preghi" of Leone, Ariosto makes them both adept at the rhetorical ploy of *efficacia*: the accomplishment of an intended result or the establishment of a state of mind in the reader by means of a logical but vivid expression.

3. We have only hinted at the conventional theatrical techniques that carry over into the narrative methods of the *Furioso*. For instance, XLIII, 118, is clearly reminiscent of the conversation in *I Suppositi* between the nurse and Damone in which he learns the truth of the matter at hand.

4. See the topos of harmonic composition discussed by Curtius, *European Literature and the Latin Middle Ages*, p. 78. Cf. also Montaigne, "each man may profit from it according to his ability," "It is the indiligent reader who loses my subject, and not I," *Essais*, II, 10; III, 9.

5. Cf. VI, 72–73; XII, 28–29, 31–32; XVI, 34–35, 78–79; XXI, 18–19; XLI, 7–8; *La Chanson de Roland*, CXXXIII–CXXXV.

6. Cf. IV, 50; V, 69; V, 9; XXI, 63; XXXII, 2; XXXIII, XLI, 46.

7. Inconstancy of the narrator, life at court, and all-conquering love receive a different inflection in the poem "Est mea nunc Glycere" (LIV).

8. The most complete histories of the impact of the *Orlando Furioso* on European literature are Walter Binni, *Storia della critica ariostesca* (Lucca: Lucentia, 1951); Aldo Borlenghi, *Ariosto* (Palermo: Palumbo, 1961); Raffaello Ramat, *La Critica ariostesca dal secolo XVI ad oggi* (Florence: La Nuova Italia, 1954); Mario Praz, *The Flaming Heart* (New York: Doubleday, 1958); Alfonso Sammut, *La Fortuna dell' Ariosto nell'Inghilterra elisabettiana;* Alexandre Cioranescu, *L'Arioste en France des origines à la fin du XVIIIᵉ siècle;* Maxime Chevalier, *Los Temas ariostescos en el romancero y la poesía española del siglo de oro* (Madrid: Castalia, 1968).

9. Allan H. Gilbert, "Spenser's Imitations from Ariosto," *PMLA* 34 (1919), pp. 225–32.

10. G. Resta, "Ariosto e i suoi personaggi," *Rivista di psicoanalisi,* 3 (1957), pp. 59–83.

Selected Bibliography

PRIMARY SOURCES

Ludovico Ariosto, Opere. Edited by Giuliano Innamorati. Bologna: Zanichelli, 1960. Helpful introduction, biography, and bibliography. Excellent critical apparatus. All quotations of the *Furioso* in the text are from this edition.

Orlando Furioso. Edited by Lanfranco Caretti. Milan and Naples: Ricciardi, 1954 (vol. 1). *Opere minori.* Edited by Caretti and Cesare Segre (vol. 2). Good essay on the affective impact of the *Furioso.* Segre's introduction has the virtue of not reducing minor works to purely derivative status. Fine comments on publication history, but critical apparatus is inadequate.

Le Commedie di Ludovico Ariosto. Edited by Michele Catalano. Bologna: Zanichelli, 1940, 2 vols. Adequate introduction and apparatus for texts in both prose and verse.

Lirica di Ludovico Ariosto. Edited by Giuseppe Fatini. Bari: Laterza, 1924. Most convenient and complete collection of Ariosto's Latin and Italian poetry. Excellent apparatus and commentary.

"Le Satire" di Ludovico Ariosto, testo critico con introduzione, facsimile e note. Edited by Giovanni Tambara. Livorno: Giusti, 1903. Useful introduction on publication history, textual problems, and variant readings.

SECONDARY SOURCES

BINNI, WALTER. *Ludovico Ariosto.* Turin: ERI, 1968. General introduction to the writer, accompanied by a useful anthology of his works.

CARDUCCI, GIOSUÈ. *Saggio su l' "Orlando Furioso."* Milan, 1881. Plays down satiric bent of the *Furioso* in order to stress its pleasing unity, but never reaches the extremes of De Sanctis or Croce.

CARNE-ROSS, DONALD. "The One and the Many." *Arion,* 5 (1966), pp. 195–234. Lucid and provocative analysis of cantos I and VIII.

CATALANO, MICHELE. *Vita di Ludovico Ariosto ricostruita su nuovi documenti.* Geneva: Olschki, 1930, 2 vols. Definitive biography based on meticulous study of archival records, social, political, and cultural milieu.

CESAREO, GIOVANNI. "La Fantasia dell Ariosto." In *Studi e richerche su la letteratura italiana*. Palermo: Sandron, 1930. Controversial polemic against Rajna, as against all efforts to diminish Ariosto's imaginative power in the face of his numerous borrowings.

CONTINI, GIANFRANCO. "Come lavorava l'Ariosto." In *Esercizi di lettura sopra autori contemporanei con un'appendice su testi non contemporanei*. Florence: Parenti, 1939. Complements and completes Debenedetti. Establishes progressive classicizing tendencies through Ariosto's stylistic emendations.

CROCE, BENEDETTO. *Ariosto, Shakespeare e Corneille*. Bari: Laterza, 1920; reprinted 1961. Very influential essay which claims that the mood of calm in the *Furioso* comes from the integration of feeling and emotion into a higher cosmic harmony.

DEBENEDETTI, SANTORRE. *I Frammenti autografi dell' "Orlando Furioso."* Turin: Chiantore, 1937. Minute analysis of Ariosto's corrections and modifications.

DE BLASI, GIORGIO. "L'Ariosto e le passioni (studio sul motivo poetico fondamentale dell'*Orlando Furioso*." *Giornale storico della letteratura italiana*, 129 and 130 (1952–53), pp. 318–62, 178–203. Rich and illuminating essay on the poet's sympathetic attitude toward the variable emotions he depicts.

DE SANCTIS, FRANCESCO. "Schemi di lezioni." in *Teoria e storia della letteratura*, edited by Benedetto Croce. Bari: Laterza, 1926, vol. 1. Although shallowness of Ariosto's emotions is exaggerated, De Sanctis' analysis of Ruggiero's character is provocative.

———. *Storia della letteratura italiana*. Naples: Morano, 1872; reprinted in Turin: Einaudi, 1966. Important study which, however, overstresses Ariosto's love of formal beauty at the expense of religious, ethical, social, or political concerns.

DURLING, ROBERT M. *The Figure of the Poet in Renaissance Epic*. Cambridge, Mass.: Harvard University Press, 1965. Incisive chapter on Ariosto that places the stance of the narrator within the context of the whole poem.

FATINI, GIUSEPPE. *Bibliografia della critica ariostea, 1510–1956*. Florence: Le Monnier, 1958. Extremely thorough compilation, although inevitably dated.

FUMAGALLI, GIUSEPPINA. *Unità fantastica dell' "Orlando Furioso."* Messina and Milan: Principato, 1933. Reduces unity of the work to the outsized emotions that move Orlando and Rodomonte. Valuable study only if it is integrated into larger unities of the *Furioso*.

Selected Bibliography

GARDNER, EDMUND. *Dukes and Poets in Ferrara*. London: Constable, 1904. Anecdotal life of Ferrara during the Este reign.

————. *The King of Court Poets: A Study of the Work, Life and Times of Ludovico Ariosto*. London: Constable, 1906. Readable and informed introduction to the writer and his work.

GIAMATTI, A. BARTLETT. *The Earthly Paradise and the Renaissance Epic*. Princeton: Princeton University Press, 1966. Close examination of Alcina's false paradise against a broad background of European Renaissance literature.

GREENE, THOMAS. *The Descent from Heaven: A Study in Epic Continuity*. New Haven: Yale University Press, 1963. An extensive consideration of the epic as a genre, through the topos of the divine messenger. Treats the descent of Silence in the *Furioso*.

MARTI, MARIO. "Ludovico Ariosto." In *Orientamenti culturali. Lettatura italiana* (1956), pp. 307–406. Exemplary introduction to the writer and his work. Looks at language, characters, and narrative technique of the *Furioso*.

MOMIGLIANO, ATTILIO. *Saggio su l' "Orlando Furioso."* Bari: Laterza, 1932; reprinted 1959. Illuminating but prolix analysis especially of Atlante, Orlando, Fiammetta, and Rodomonte episodes. Continues but corrects Crocean themes.

MONTANO, ROCCO. *Follia e saggezza nel "Furioso" e nell'elogio di Erasmo*. Naples: Humanitas, 1942. Important and underrated examination of realism, humor, and irony of Ariosto in a broad and helpful Renaissance context.

L'OTTAVA D'ORO. Milan and Verona: Mondadori, 1933. Anthology of critical articles, mainly on the *Furioso*, of unequal value.

PIROMALLI, ANTONIO. *Motivi e forme della poesia di Ludovico Ariosto*. Messina and Florence: D'Anna, 1954. Basing his case on the text itself, Piromalli discusses the attitude of the narrator toward the poem and its Renaissance setting.

POOL, FRANCO. *Interpretazione dell' "Orlando Furioso."* Florence: La Nuova Italia, 1968. Limpid analysis of major episodes in the work.

RAJNA, PIO. *Le Fonti dell' "Orlando Furioso."* Florence: Sansoni, 1876. Aside from the untenable proposition that the "originality" of Ariosto's poem is inversely proportional to the many sources it draws upon, this is a major scholarly work.

SANTINI, EMILIO. *La Poesia dell' "Orlando Furioso" ed esercizi di lettura ariostesca*. Palermo: Denaro e La Fauci, 1954. Collection of articles on various subjects relating to Ariosto's work.

SAPEGNO, NATALINO. "Ludovico Ariosto." In *Compendio di storia della letteratura italiana*. Florence: La Nuova Italia, 1939, vol. 2. Tightly balanced introduction to the man and his work.

Index

Index

Index of Characters in *Orlando Furioso*